From

SKEPTIC *to*
CHRISTIAN

•

*persuaded
by the
evidence*

From

SKEPTIC to
CHRISTIAN

•

*persuaded
by the
evidence*

GORDON PEARCE

WINEPRESS WP PUBLISHING

Packaged by WinePress Publishing, PO Box 428, Enumclaw, WA 98022. The views expressed or implied in this work do not necessarily reflect those of WinePress Publishing. Ultimate design, content, and editorial accuracy of this work are the responsibilities of the author.

ISBN 1-57921-382-0
Library of Congress Catalog Card Number: 20011088922

To Pastor Hap Brahams,
  who showed me the path,
And to my wife, Marlise,
  who held my hand along the way.

Table of Contents

Preface

✝

Ask the average Christian, "Why do you believe in the New Testament?" He or she may well fumble for an answer. Then ask the average skeptic, "Why *don't* you believe in the New Testament?" He or she may also fumble for an answer. This book is written for both kinds of people. It confronts skeptics with an array of solid facts from which they can reexamine their position. And it gives Christians ammunition with which they can defend their faith. Its message is simple: *The historical truth of the gospel accounts is supported by a rational evaluation of the evidence.*

The idea for this book was born late in 1980. I had almost finished a seven-year study of Christian evidence, aimed at discovering a personal belief in God. One evening a friend commented that he belonged to a Christian church, attended it regularly, and even served on the finance committee. But then he posed a surprising question: "Gordon, you don't really believe all that stuff in the Bible really happened, do you?" During the next few days I reflected on his doubt about the historical truth of the New Testament gospels. Then an idea began to take shape: Perhaps I should write down a summary of my own study of the evidence and offer it to people such as my friend. This book is the result.

My credentials as a Christian author do not come from academic preparation. I was educated in economics and law, receiving both degrees from UCLA. After completing military service and working several years for a Los Angeles law firm, I joined the law department of Western Airlines. Nine years later I accepted a position as vice president and general attorney (later, general counsel) of San Diego Gas & Electric Company, where I remained until retiring from the practice of law.

Because of this professional background, I was accustomed to the process of sifting through evidence and drawing conclusions from it.

From Skeptic to Christian: Persuaded by the Evidence has emerged from my protracted research into scholarly books and articles. As a layman's survey of the evidence, it supports the historical reliability of the New Testament gospels and of their central character, Jesus of Nazareth. In writing this book, I tried to stand back and take a broad perspective, exploring highways and byways but avoiding repeated detours into scholarly details and theological jargon. The central objective was to summarize the evidence intelligibly and to evaluate it fairly.

An extraordinary array of relatives, friends, and strangers gave generously of their time and talents in reviewing the manuscript for accuracy and readability. Some were skeptics. Some were wordsmiths. Some were pastors. And some were scholars. Most of their suggestions have been incorporated, and the book is a far better product because of their willingness to lend a hand. So, at a very personal level, I offer profound thanks to Alan, Bob, Carol, Casey, Charles, Colleen, Corinne, Harris, Hunter, Jim, Joe, Joe, Lew, Lyle, Marlise, Patricia, Paul, Rick, Sam, Scott, and Stanley!

All Biblical quotations are from the New International Version (NIV) unless otherwise specified. For ease of reference, each footnote is positioned on the page to which it relates. Citations to the Bible's sixty-six books are in the customary form of book, chapter, and verse, e.g., Job 14:14 (from the Old Testament) and Matthew 22:37 and 1 Peter 3:15 (from the New Testament).

Solvang, California
February 2001

Chapter One

†

THREE SERIOUS QUESTIONS

SETTING THE STAGE

At age ten I was regularly attending Sunday School. At age twenty I had changed into an ardent atheist, believing that God did not exist and diligently staying away from churches. By age thirty, as a young attorney, I had become a comfortable agnostic. At age forty I was still an agnostic. But by age fifty I was becoming intellectually convinced of two things: first, that the New Testament gospels accurately recorded the life of Jesus and, second, that Jesus had probably been resurrected from the dead—something only God could have done. By age sixty I was fully convinced of these two facts and had used them as a springboard for a short step of faith. I had come to believe that Jesus is God's son, that his teaching must be taken seriously, and that faith in him is the passport to eternal life with God. In other words, I had become a Christian. This book describes the evidence and reasoning which led me to that faith.

My early atheism had its roots in Thomas Paine's *Age of Reason*. Paine was a deist. He believed that God created the universe, but he denied that God performed miracles in human history, and he disbelieved Jesus' claim to be God in human form. Paine's book made sense to me at the time. But I incorrectly interpreted it as an argument that God didn't exist.

During my years as an atheist, identifying a faith in God proved elusive. For me, the mystery of the universe could not be clarified by substituting an equally mysterious "God." I became satisfied that the universe had always existed, a theory that was considered plausible in those days. I was fond of telling religious friends, "You can't create a faith if your mind isn't convinced of it, and mine isn't. If God is out there, he must surely dislike hypocrites more than he dislikes sincere unbelievers."

In spite of this attitude, I continued to vaguely understand the importance of searching for God, even though I had not yet discovered that the search could be predicated on a rational review of existing evidence.

Around age twenty-seven, I veered from atheism to agnosticism. It was more "intellectually honest." It was also insidiously comfortable. In my mind (1) there was no need to take a position at either end of the atheist/believer spectrum, (2) the risk of going to hell was minimal, since only atheists went there, and (3) the prospect of heaven remained open, because sincere agnostics could be "good people." But I failed to realize that my *refusal to make* a decision was, in effect, a decision *against* the existence of God. My attitude illustrated the false sense of security that lulls agnostics into quiet apathy. They can just drift through life without thinking seriously about theological matters. Fortunately, I never slipped all the way into that frame of mind. Although I didn't do any real searching, and never attended church, I did continue to acknowledge the *possibility* that God exists.

In 1974, at age forty-five, my transformation began. It happened soon after I started playing tennis with Harry "Hap" Brahams, the new pastor of the La Jolla Presbyterian Church in San Diego, California. I quickly learned that he was the sort of player who could regularly defeat (but not quite humiliate) me. I also learned that he was a thoughtful, sensible, articulate man. So, nudged by something deep inside, and with certain trepidation, I asked if he would be willing to talk theology with me. Predictably, he was pleased to do so. Thus, under Hap's tutelage, I began a serious, seven-year study to find out whether God was real.

At the outset, Hap pointed out that my philosophical ruminations about God had not produced any concrete results. So he suggested that an investigation of Jesus might be a more useful approach, because "Christians believe that Jesus was God in the flesh and that his real footprints on the dusty paths of Palestine can be studied historically." My slightly arrogant response was, "If God exists, which I doubt, I don't need an intermediary to deal with him." Hap laughed, commenting that my intermittent reflections about God had gotten me nowhere during the past twenty-five years. He asked what I would have to lose, other than some time, by checking out the historical Jesus as a means of discovering God. I had no rational escape from this logic. If Jesus could be studied empirically as an historical figure, why not give it a try? So I decided to embark on the journey, keeping in mind Hap's two threshold admonitions: First, I should not become discouraged by the likelihood that my path would be long and arduous, and, second, I should not become intimidated by anyone who might someday look upon me as a "second-class" Christian for not having had a sudden, emotional conversion. These were wise warnings, which I often found helpful in the years ahead.

From the very beginning, I realized two important points. First, the reliability of the New Testament documents was critical. People living in Palestine nearly two thousand years ago had the opportunity to actually see and hear Jesus in person, or at least to talk with other people who had seen and heard him. They could form their own opinions about him from first-hand evidence. Today, none of us has that advantage. Instead, our only comprehensive sources of information about Jesus' life, teachings, death, and resurrection are the New Testament gospels (Matthew, Mark, Luke, and John).[1] However, in order to form a belief about Jesus on the basis of four ancient books, a modern reader must become satisfied that they are verifiably accurate accounts of who Jesus was and what he taught. If the Gospels pass this test, then Jesus can be studied, and conclusions about him can be reached.

----

[1] The four gospels differ from the other New Testament books, which, except for the book of Acts (Luke's historical account of the early Church's growth during its first thirty years), are mostly interpretive and contain few explicit references to the facts of Jesus' life.

The second important point I realized was that, in searching for evidence to support a Christian faith, the pivotal event was Jesus' claimed resurrection from the dead.[2] If it really happened, as a matter of historical fact, then the only rational explanation must be that God exists, that he performed this supernatural act within human history, and that he would not have done so unless Jesus was a uniquely different sort of person.

So I made a bargain with myself: If I ever came to the conclusion that the resurrection more probably happened than not, then I would have to accept the identity of Jesus and the existence of God. In formulating this bargain about the historicity of the resurrection, I chose not to demand *overwhelming* evidence. Instead, I decided that my eventual conclusion about the resurrection should be based on a *preponderance* of the evidence, i.e., evidence supporting a probability of at least fifty-one percent. I felt that this approach would avoid the pitfall of gambling my eternal future on personal bias rather than the simple weight of the evidence.

Seven years later, after having slowly come to realize that the New Testament gospels are reliable accounts of a man who really existed and of events that truly happened, I concluded that God did indeed raise Jesus from the dead. It was an actual historical event in time and space. So the condition of my self-imposed bargain had been satisfied. The implications of this situation quickly permeated my innermost thoughts, and, during a few intense days in early 1981, I found myself poised for a step of Christian faith. The step itself consisted of nothing more than my satisfied head telling my nervous heart to "get with the program." I don't know exactly how it happened, but my heart suddenly embraced the idea. During the Easter season, I publicly professed my belief that

---

[2] The word *resurrect* means bringing back to life. It differs from *resuscitate,* which is normally used to describe restoration to consciousness or vigor, although it also means restoration to life. The New Testament gospels claim that, when Jesus was resurrected from the dead, he came back in such a form that he would not die again. This distinguishes his resurrection from other biblical stories (and many modern stories) describing people who have been resuscitated from clinical deaths, but who all eventually die a final death.

Jesus was God's son and that God had raised him from the dead. Hap then baptized me.

It had been a long—and fruitful—walk. But the best still lay ahead. Within months I was acquiring the confidence to undertake church and corporate projects that once would have panicked me. At the same time I was gaining the strength to cope with career and health crises that once would have overwhelmed me. In a very real way, my new faith had already started to pay definable, demonstrable dividends.

Chapters two through eight of this book describe the evidentiary foundation from which my step of faith was launched. Each piece of that evidence helped to destroy some key assumptions that had given birth to my skepticism. During all my years as a skeptic, I had inexplicably taken these assumptions for granted, never subjecting them to careful investigation. Yet, upon examination through the lens of evidence, every one of them turned out to be wrong. For instance, I had long assumed that:

- Many of the Bible stories were mythological. Wrong!
- The New Testament gospels were written long after the alleged events and were therefore unreliable. Wrong!
- Our English New Testament was the result of many translations and was therefore replete with inaccuracies. Wrong!
- The Bible was full of contradictions that destroyed its credibility. Wrong!
- Many Christians were arrogant and patronizing, so the Christian "faith" couldn't possibly be worthwhile. Wrong!
- "God" was unknowable, so it was pointless to believe he exists. Wrong!

The weight of the evidence led me to abandon these mistaken assumptions, thereby setting the stage for my acceptance of God's existence, Jesus' claims, and heaven's reality.

Turning now toward an examination of the evidence, we will start with a simple statement of the three serious issues that first motivated me to undertake the journey.

STATING THE QUESTIONS

We all live somewhere: in a country, in a state, in a region. We all fit into a slot on the economic spectrum: wealthy, middle class, poor. We all belong to an age group: elderly, middle-aged, young. We all have a gender: male or female. In a word, we humans are diverse. But we do share at least one common characteristic: All of us, no matter who we are or where we live, face daily questions that demand answers and decisions. The questions vary in importance. Some have serious consequences (Should I change jobs?). Others are less significant (Where should I spend my next vacation?). Many are virtually trivial (What vegetable should we serve for dinner tonight?).

However, it seems to me that every person's short list of the "most serious questions" should include three vital issues:

- Does God exist?
- If so, is there life with God after death?
- If there is, how do I get from this life to that one?

These three questions confront the entire human race and ought not to be evaded. Every one of us should take them seriously and deal with them squarely, minimizing our own personal pride and intellectual prejudice. The task of searching for answers deserves complete openness to any possible outcome—even one that contradicts deeply-held presuppositions.

Our ancestors have certainly been serious about the questions. God's existence has been a vital issue for the human race far back into the mists of prehistory. Life after death has been pondered by such diverse minds as ancient Job[3] and modern existentialists. And getting into some sort of blissful afterlife has long been a central religious theme.

This book is addressed to people who are intellectually skeptical about things like the existence of God and the reality/accessi-

---

[3] Job 14:14.

bility of life after death. These people can be atheists (who deny that God exists), or they can be agnostics (who deny the reality of any *persuasive evidence* that God exists, but not the *possibility* that he exists). They can also be people who believe in some sort of supreme being and in life after death, but who reject the Judeo/Christian concept of a personal God and the Christian belief in Jesus' divinity.[4] For convenience, I have used the term "skeptic" to cover all three groups.

REALIZING WHY THE QUESTIONS ARE IMPORTANT

Before exploring the substance of the three serious questions, and possible paths toward answers, one preliminary issue must be faced: Why should skeptical people attach any particular importance to questions about God's existence, about life after death, and, in particular, about the Christian claim that a relationship with God must come through Jesus?

The reason is stark and straightforward. If the skeptic is right and the Christian is wrong, then they are both likely to experience "nothingness" after death. The Christian will have been deluded during his lifetime. But his erroneous belief will not have lost him anything, because his consciousness will probably cease forever at the time of death. By contrast, if the skeptic is wrong and the Christian is right, the dead skeptic will consciously experience eternal separation from God. His erroneous belief will have caused him to irretrievably lose everything forever.[5]

---

[4] Chapter ten includes a discussion of the "intolerant and arrogant" Christian claim that Jesus is the only avenue to God.

[5] Pascal's Wager divided atheism and faith into four logical possibilities: (1) God does not exist/you do not believe, (2) God does not exist/you do believe, (3) God exists/you do not believe, and (4) God exists/you do believe. Neither (1) nor (2) offers a chance of winning the prize of eternal life, since there is no such prize. Number three offers the only chance of losing the prize, and (4) offers the only chance of winning it. So faith is a "no-lose" bet, and atheism is a "no-win" bet. J. P. Moreland and Kai Nielsen, *Does God Exist?* (Nashville, TN: Thomas Nelson, 1990), pp. 289-290.

So it is plain, common sense to recognize the eternal importance of the three questions and to undertake a serious, diligent search for answers. This does not mean that common sense demands the *adoption* of religious faith. Rather, it means that common sense demands the *investigation* of religious faith. To put the matter bluntly, procrastination and apathy are dangerous. Any one of us can die at any moment. When that happens, all our plans to "someday" search for answers become instantly irrelevant.

Apathy seldom starts with a conscious decision to avoid thinking about something. Rather, it typically grows from recurring little pragmatic decisions to put other things higher on one's personal priority list. In western society these "other things" can take many forms: competition for success in the workplace, scramble for social status, quest for academic prestige, pursuit of material possessions and pleasures, and even daily drifts into cyberspace and television land. All these things share one common characteristic: By focusing our attention on the world around us, they push aside thoughts of a supernatural God and life after death. Even if such thoughts do occasionally intrude, many people proceed no further than the comforting notion that "if there's a heaven, I'll get there because I'm a good person." This pleasant idea may seem reasonable. But it might also be false. So the sensible thing to do, considering the awful consequence of being wrong, is to carve out enough time from one's daily life to evaluate the three important questions seriously and thoughtfully. Ducking or delaying the issue is risky.

So is lip-service Christianity. A lip-service Christian attends church and gets a warm, fuzzy feeling every Sunday morning, but he or she does not firmly believe that the New Testament characters (especially Jesus) ever really existed or that the New Testament events ever really happened. Such a Christian implicitly assumes that reliable historical evidence is either unimportant or does not exist. So he never takes the time to intelligently investigate whether evidence is actually available. At the very least, this Christian has abandoned his New Testament obligation to talk knowledgeably with skeptics and to gently and respectfully give answers to people who ask about his faith.[6] If Christians are unable to explain why the New Testament gospels are true, then their skeptical friends will be less motivated to investigate the validity of the Christian faith.

This book describes a path toward answers for the three serious questions. The path is paved with significant evidence supporting the historical accuracy of the New Testament gospels and of their primary figure, Jesus of Nazareth. The evidence is presented in the form of a comprehensive survey that avoids tedious, scholarly style and steers clear of long, complex analyses. To have probed exhaustively into all the academic and theological nuances would have severely tested the depth of my own knowledge, as well as the patience of readers. More importantly, it would have obscured the overall picture of the evidence by a text that was much too long and far too cumbersome.

The rest of the book is organized along the following lines: Chapter two proposes a path toward answers to the three serious questions, emphasizing commonsense principles by which the historical evidence should be evaluated.

Chapter three summarizes various ancient, non-Christian writings that refer to Jesus and his followers as actual people who played real roles on the stage of human history.

Chapter four describes the origin of the New Testament gospels, starting with their translation into modern English and then working backward to their derivation from old Greek papyrus manuscripts and from the oral tradition that preceded the long-lost original gospel manuscripts.

Chapters five and six review the evidence, primarily archaeological, that corroborates the detailed accounts in the Gospels and in Luke's book of Acts (which is a continuation of his gospel). The mosaic of evidence in these two chapters supports the historical truth of many scenes on the New Testament tapestry.

Chapter seven focuses on evidence corroborating the gospel claim that Jesus was resurrected from the dead.

---

[6] 1 Peter 3:15.

Chapter eight presents the current status of research on the Shroud of Turin—a controversial piece of old linen that is perhaps a forensic fingerprint of the resurrection event itself.

Chapter nine addresses the nagging notion that Christianity just doesn't satisfy instinctive feelings of common sense, even for people who are satisfied with the factual foundation of the gospel record.

Chapter ten explains how six common impediments to a step of Christian faith can be moved aside.

Finally, the Epilogue touches briefly on some scriptural standards of conduct and some personal rewards for people who take the step of Christian faith.

Chapter Two

✝

A Path Toward Answers

Once a person realizes that questions about God and life after death are critically important issues, he or she must find a way to respond. While the importance of the questions can provide a *motive* for seeking answers, it does not illuminate the *path* for discovering those answers. Such a path can be mapped out only after the person develops a clear sense of the direction in which he or she must start traveling. This direction will vary from person to person.

Finding Answers

For some people, the very existence of the universe (with its countless stars and galaxies) and of the earth (with its vast array of plant, animal, and human life) are sufficient to demonstrate that God exists. He is the uncaused first cause of it all, since the "big bang" when the universe started could not have caused itself.

For other people, the design and operation of the universe (including life on Earth) prove the existence of God. They understand that without an orderly design the universe would be haphazard and chaotic. Science itself would be an impossibility. So they conclude that some orderly force must have created the design,[1] and they identify this force as God.

---

[1] This viewpoint has received support from a professor of biochemistry, who showed that things like the complex chemical engines within living cells couldn't be explained by evolutionary concepts of random variation and natural selection. Instead, they are the product of intelligent design. Michael J. Behe, *Darwin's Black Box* (New York: The Free Press, 1996).

For still others, the perceived existence of moral values, which cannot be explained by anything that happens in the universe, demonstrate God's existence. They define him as the transcendent source of these values.

Many people, however, have no need for these sorts of intellectual analyses. They may have been raised in religious environments that made it easy and natural to believe in God and in life after death. Or they may have received some kind of vision or revelation that God exists. Or they may have had some other sort of religious experience.

For all these types of people, belief in God and heaven is not difficult.

But many others do not find the matter quite so clear. They encounter philosophical obstacles in accepting a supreme being who cannot be seen, heard, or touched. Or they experience moral outrage at the "unfair" idea that anyone who rejects Jesus will be denied access to God and heaven. They may even quit thinking about the entire subject. For such people, the best way to pursue or rekindle their thoughts about God and heaven may be to temporarily bypass the philosophical and moral issues and to undertake an historical investigation of this man Jesus. I followed precisely such a path in my own search for answers.

EVALUATING THE EVIDENCE

Christianity is not a faith that captures a person's heart while demanding that he disregard his intellect. In fact, according to the New Testament, Jesus himself told a legal expert that the greatest commandment is to love God "with all your heart and with all your soul and with all your *mind*."[2]

But before mobilizing our minds for an evaluation of the historical evidence, one preliminary comment is in order. Any person who undertakes a study of the Gospels should get hold of a good modern translation of the Bible. Two examples are the *New Inter-*

---

[2] Matthew 22:37; (emphasis added.)

national Version (NIV) and the *New Revised Standard Version* (NRSV). The old King James Version, with its rich poetic imagery, was written in sixteenth-century Elizabethan language that is often difficult to understand today. By contrast, modern translations are quite readable and comprehensible. Moreover, compared to the meager resources available 400 years ago, the new translations are based on a more reliable collection of ancient manuscripts and on an improved knowledge of the ancient everyday Greek language in which the New Testament manuscripts were originally written. So the modern translations tend to be more accurate than the King James Version.

An historical investigation of Jesus—or of any other ancient person—must deal with two types of evidence: *direct* (such as written accounts that purport to describe real people and events) and *circumstantial* (such as archaeological artifacts, from which logical inferences can be drawn). Circumstantial evidence is often more reliable than written documents, since it cannot be as readily altered or fabricated. Debates over particular archaeological artifacts seldom involve authenticity. Instead, the arguments typically revolve around the strength of the inferences that can be drawn from the items. For example, a marble slab was discovered many years ago in Nazareth. It bears a first-century Roman imperial decree imposing capital punishment on grave robbers. As a piece of evidence, the slab is authentic. But debate exists over the strength of an inference: Was the imperial decree issued in response to early non-Christian claims that Jesus' body had been stolen from its tomb? The substance of this issue will be reviewed in chapter seven.

Turning now from *types* of evidence to the *procedures* for evaluating it, four commonsense principles should govern the process.

First, the factual statements of any ancient writer ought to be taken at face value unless there is reason to think that he (1) lied, (2) exaggerated, (3) had inadequate evidence for his statements, (4) was writing metaphorically or allegorically, or (5) was writing legends or fiction. This "face value presumption" is a recognized cornerstone of historical investigation.[3] It undergirds our judgments about the reliability of *current* books and articles concerning historical events, and it applies equally to evaluations of *ancient* historical writings—such as the New Testament gospels. In fact, much of our knowledge about ancient secular history is derived from nothing more than the writings of ancient authors. Without the face value presumption, they would have to be discarded as reliable records—something few historians would be willing to do.

With regard to the gospel accounts, the face value presumption cannot be dodged by complaints that the writers were biased. An author's primary prejudices—and even some of his subtle ones— are usually identifiable and can be taken into account when evaluating the historical accuracy of his work. For example, if some future scholar were to reconstruct the events occurring in Germany between 1933 and 1945, a primary source could be William L. Shirer's book, *The Rise and Fall of the Third Reich*.[4] Our future scholar would take into account Mr. Shirer's introductory statement:

> . . .my own prejudices. . .creep through the pages of this book. . .Nevertheless, . . .no incidents, scenes or quotations stem from the imagination; all are based on documents, the testimony of eye-witnesses or my own personal observation.[5]

Gospel author Luke makes a comparable claim at the outset of his account.[6]

---

[3] Craig L. Blomberg, *The Historical Reliability of the Gospels* (Downers Grove, IL: Inter-Varsity, 1987), p. 240; R. T. France, *The Evidence for Jesus* (Downers Grove, IL: InterVarsity, 1986), pp. 102–103.

[4] Reprinted with the permission of Simon & Schuster from *The Rise and Fall of the Third Reich* by William L. Shirer. Copyright 1959, 1960, 1987, 1988 by William L. Shirer.

[5] Ibid., p. xii.

[6] Luke 1:1–4.

The crux of the matter is that an author's personal attitudes and opinions do not automatically disqualify him as a reliable historical source. Illustrations abound. Dwight Eisenhower's biases (as the commander of Allied forces in Europe during World War II) can certainly be factored into any reading of his book *Crusade in Europe*. And Winston Churchill's prejudices (as prime minister of Great Britain during World War II) can be filtered out when judging the reliability of his six-volume *The Second World War*. Or, to take an ancient example, Julius Caesar's partialities can be taken into consideration by anyone who uses his commentaries to learn about the Gallic wars in 58–51 B.C.[7]

The New Testament gospels are equally open to filtration for bias. So skeptics cannot legitimately skirt the face value presumption of gospel accuracy by simply declaring that the authors were biased in their beliefs about Jesus.

Second, conclusions should be derived from the cumulative weight of *all* the evidence, not just from selected parts of *some* of it. The amount of evidence from two thousand years ago is not abundant. Anyone who evaluates it should avoid the temptation to draw conclusions from only one or two pieces while ignoring other pieces that are in conflict. We surely would not have much confidence in a botanist who describes an entire forest by examining only two or three of its many species of trees.

These first two principles are sometimes disregarded by radical and well-publicized "Jesus" scholars, who are reluctant to take the Gospels at face value and who focus instead on selected slices of evidence that fit their own preconceived theories.[8]

Third, stories of miracles and divine intervention should not be dismissed as fantasy just because we have no scientific explanation for them. To do so would violate the very essence of scientific

---

[7] To avoid the confusion of unfamiliar terminology, I have used the traditional designations of "B.C." and "A.D.," rather than today's scholarly abbreviations of "B.C.E." (before the common era) and "C.E." (common era).

[8] Numerous examples are reviewed by Ben Witherington III in *The Jesus Quest* (Downers Grove, IL: InterVarsity Press, 1995).

inductive method, which does not dismiss any working hypothesis (like God's existence) to explain an alleged event (like a miracle) merely because no living person has seen it happen. Much of today's technology and modern scientific knowledge would have been defined as sheer fiction by intelligent people living three hundred years ago.

Fourth, historical evidence must be evaluated in terms of *probabilities*, not certainties. A wise investigator is never afraid to say, "I don't know," instead of drawing unwarranted conclusions from inadequate evidence. Even for Christians, "I don't know" is a perfectly acceptable answer when they face vexing questions about difficult statements in the New Testament writings. And when Christians are considering the historical basis for their faith, *doubt* should never be an obscene word. The evidence simply does not provide absolute answers to every question about the historical picture of Jesus. But when looked at in terms of probabilities, the evidence furnishes a solid foundation for the New Testament's description of him. Modern skeptics can take comfort from Thomas, one of the disciples, who insisted on seeing the nail marks in Jesus' hands before believing that the resurrection had actually happened.[9] The lesson is not that Thomas doubted. Rather, it is that he was open to the evidence and was willing to believe when confronted by it.

In addition to the two types of evidence and the four principles used in evaluating it, several scholarly disciplines come into play when judging the authenticity and accuracy of the New Testament gospels. One is paleography, the study and interpretation of ancient documents by analyzing the forms of writing that appear on them. Paleography aids in authenticating and dating the New Testament documents. Another discipline is archaeology, the study of material remains from past human lives and cultures. It helps in corroborating the historical and geographical accuracy of the New Testament accounts. Even astronomy (the study of celestial bodies

---

[9] John 20:24–29.

and outer space) gets into the act, allowing us to test the Star of Bethlehem story.

Throughout any investigation of the historical Jesus, Thomas's attitude of healthy skepticism will furnish good seasoning to sharpen the search. But skepticism should always be tested by common sense—an ingredient that helps avoid the temptation to devise complex and speculative analyses which sidestep the plain factual statements in the Gospels. Such analyses typically presuppose that authors of religious history cannot be trusted. If such a presupposition persists, then healthy skepticism can be reduced to a scholarly fetish. It may even degenerate into cynicism, which, like naive gullibility, will prevent honest investigation.

STEPPING FROM EVIDENCE TO FAITH

If a person becomes satisfied that the Gospels accurately describe an historical person—a man named Jesus, who lived, taught, died, and was probably resurrected from the dead—then it is only a short step of faith to arrive at a belief in God and heaven. A long leap is not required. But the short step is vital, because mere intellectual agreement with the evidence does not constitute faith. What the evidence does supply is the intellectual platform from which to take that step of faith. The step itself transforms a probability into a firm and threefold belief: (1) God exists, (2) there is life after death, and (3) Jesus is the door to a relationship and eternal life with God.

Thus our three original questions will have been answered, partly by a foundation of historical evidence, and partly by the willingness to take a confident step of faith. This step allows us to be "sure of what we hope for and certain of what we do not see."[10] From then on, the content of Jesus' teachings can become the focus of further study, leading toward a clearer understanding of how to spend life on Earth before entering life eternal.

---

[10] Hebrews 11:1.

Chapter Three

✝

REFERENCES TO JESUS AND THE CHRISTIANS IN ANCIENT WRITINGS

Before we explore whether the New Testament gospels are reliable records of actual historical events, one threshold question is in order: Was Jesus of Nazareth a real person who lived and died, or was he a legendary figure contrived in the imaginations of the gospel authors? Nearly every modern scholar, whether secular or religious, acknowledges that he actually existed. But is there any independent evidence to that effect? Yes. A number of ancient, non-Christian writings refer to Jesus and his followers by name. In various degrees of detail, they confirm the scholarly opinion that he was a true historical person.

ROMAN WRITINGS

Several ancient Roman historians and officials refer to Jesus and his followers. The references are not extensive. However, at the height of Rome's power in the first century A.D., the comings and goings of an itinerant Jewish rabbi on the remote eastern fringes of the empire would hardly have been front-page news. In fact, it is surprising that Jesus was even mentioned at all in Roman records of the time. But indeed he was. And these references provide independent confirmation that he was a real, live figure in the turbulent world of first-century Palestine.

Tacitus. Born about A.D. 55, Cornelius Tacitus was a distinguished Roman historian and a friend of Pliny the Younger. Around A.D. 112 he served as governor (proconsul) of Asia, just after Pliny had been governor of neighboring Bithynia (the north-central part of modern Turkey). Several years later Tacitus wrote his two most famous books of Roman history: *Annals* (covering the period A.D.14–68) and *Histories* (covering the period A.D. 68–70). In *Annals* he described the great fire of Rome (A.D. 64) and the emperor Nero's effort to shift the blame from himself to the Roman Christians. Tacitus wrote that:

> Nero fastened the guilt and inflicted the most exquisite tortures on a class. . .called Christians by the populace. Christus, from whom the name had its origin, suffered the extreme penalty during the reign of Tiberius at the hands of one of our procurators, Pontius Pilatus, and a most mischievous superstition, thus checked for the moment, again broke out not only in Judaea, the first source of the evil, but even in Rome.[1]

Tacitus was writing about eighty-five years after Jesus' crucifixion, and we frankly do not know the source of his information. He probably would not have relied on the accounts of the Christians, whom he seems to have openly despised. Most likely he utilized the official reports that Pilate must have periodically sent to Rome. As a distinguished Roman citizen, Tacitus would have had access to the archives where any such reports were filed.

Unfortunately, those archives have long since vanished from history. Not a single report, no matter what the subject, has come down to us from any Roman governor of Judea. But such reports did exist at one time. Around A.D. 150 an early Christian leader, Justin Martyr, wrote a long letter to the Roman emperor Antoninus Pius. In it he mentioned Jesus' crucifixion and the division of his clothing among the Roman soldiers. Justin noted that the emperor could verify the facts from the "Acts of what was done under Pontius

---

[1] Tacitus, *Annals* 15.44, Great Books of the Western World, vol. 15, trans. Alfred John Church and William Jackson Brodribb (Chicago, IL: Encyclopaedia Britannica, 1952), p. 168. Reprinted from Great Books of the Western World © 1952, 1990 Encyclopaedia Britannica, Inc.

Pilate."[2] Such an invitation to a Roman emperor would have been quite risky if no record of the "Acts" had existed.

Suetonius. Another well-known Roman historian who referred to Jesus was Suetonius. Born about A.D. 69, he, like Tacitus, was a friend of Pliny the Younger. Serving for a time as private secretary to the emperor Hadrian, Suetonius wrote what we would today call biographies. His only surviving work is entitled *The Twelve Caesars*. Written around A.D. 120, it covers the emperors from Julius Caesar to Domitian.

Suetonius includes in his biography of Nero a brief reference to punishments that were "inflicted on the Christians, a sect professing a new and mischievous religious belief."[3] This is probably an abbreviated reference to the aftermath of the great fire, more fully described by Tacitus. It confirms that Rome possessed an active community of practicing Christians within thirty-five years after Jesus' crucifixion.

Pliny the Younger. One other Roman mentioned Jesus. Pliny the Younger, born around A.D. 62, was an orator and statesman. He held various official positions, including the governorship of Bithynia, where he died in about A.D. 113.

Pliny was an inveterate letter writer. Many of his letters, written from Bithynia, were addressed to the emperor Trajan. In one of them Pliny sought advice about dealing with the local Christians, who refused to demonstrate reverence for Caesar's image. The issue may have been brought to the governor's attention by the sellers of sacrificial animals for pagan temples, who complained that their business was being jeopardized by the Christian movement. Pliny commented to the emperor that the Christians met regularly and sang a hymn "to Christ as to a god."[4]

---

[2] Justin Martyr, "First Apology" 35, *Early Christian Fathers*, trans. and ed. Cyril C. Richardson (New York: Macmillan, 1970), p. 264.

[3] Suetonius, "Nero" 16, *The Twelve Caesars*, trans. Robert Graves, rev. ed. (London: Penguin Group, 1979), p. 221.

[4] Quoted by F. F. Bruce in *New Testament History* (New York: Doubleday, 1971), p. 165.

This letter tells us nothing about Jesus' life and teachings. But it does allow us to conclude that, within about eighty years after his crucifixion, the Christians in Pliny's province believed that Jesus had been a real person—one who was also divine.

OTHER GENTILE WRITINGS

Thallus. Apart from the three Roman writers discussed above, another gentile author, Thallus, may have been familiar with the accounts of Jesus as early as A.D. 52 (although one scholar places the date around A.D. 100). We know nothing about Thallus, except that he wrote a history of the eastern Mediterranean area, starting with the Trojan War (which probably took place around 1200 B.C.).

Thallus's history, except for eight fragments, has long since disappeared. But around A.D. 221, it was referred to by Julius Africanus, an early Christian writer on chronology.[5] In describing the darkness that allegedly occurred when Jesus was crucified, Africanus says that Thallus had explained it as a solar eclipse. Africanus disagreed with this explanation. But the important point is that his reference to Thallus gives us reason to think that the story of Jesus' crucifixion was known in the Mediterranean area as early as twenty years after it happened.

Mara bar Serapion. Sometime after A.D. 73 (how much later is not known) a man named Mara bar Serapion penned a letter to his son.[6] Written in Syriac, it is now preserved in the British Museum. In urging his son to pursue wisdom, Mara bar Serapion noted that people who persecute wise men often fall victims to misfortune themselves. He illustrated this point with specific examples, one of which almost certainly was a reference to Jesus. He asked his son what advantage the Jews gained from executing their "wise

---

[5] F. F. Bruce, *The New Testament Documents*, 5th rev. ed. (Grand Rapids, MI: Eerdmans, 1994), p. 113.

[6] Described by F. F. Bruce in *Jesus and Christian Origins Outside the New Testament* (Grand Rapids, MI: Eerdmans, 1974), pp. 30–31.

king," since immediately afterward their kingdom was abolished.[7] He pointed out that the "wise king" lived on in his teachings.

Lucian of Samosata. Around A.D. 170 Lucian, a Greek satirical writer, wrote sarcastically about the early Christians.

> [They]. . .worship a man to this day—the distinguished personage who introduced their novel rites, and was crucified on that account. . .You see, these misguided creatures start with the general conviction that they are immortal for all time, which explains the contempt of death. . .[They] worship the crucified sage, and live after his laws. All this they take quite on faith.[8]

Lucian's disdainful remarks confirm that, by the mid-second century, Jesus and his movement had become well known in literate, skeptical circles around the Mediterranean area.

THE JEWISH HISTORIAN JOSEPHUS

Unlike the early Christians, many of whom had converted from Judaism, the majority of Jews rejected the notion that Jesus was their long-awaited messiah. So any Jewish historical writing from the first century would very likely represent the work of an author who rejected Jesus' claims about being divine. In that sense, the evidence of Jewish writings is just as independent as the work of Roman and other gentile writers.

We are fortunate to have available today the writings of a prolific Jewish historian named Josephus. Born in A.D. 37, he became a Pharisee and served as the Jewish military commander in Galilee during the war against the Romans, which started in A.D. 66. When the Romans overran Galilee, he went into hiding with some local townspeople. Declining to follow their example, Josephus did not

---

[7] In A.D. 66 the Romans began to crush a Jewish rebellion, and four years later they destroyed Jerusalem and its temple.

[8] Lucian, The Death of Peregrine, 11–13, quoted in Josh McDowell & Bill Wilson, He Walked Among Us (San Bernardino, CA: Here's Life Publishers, 1988), pp. 53–54.

commit suicide. Instead, he surrendered and later served the Romans as a mediator and interpreter. He ingratiated himself to Vespasian, the Roman commander, who soon became emperor and brought Josephus to Rome. Josephus even adopted Vespasian's family name, Flavius. Many ancient Jews considered him a traitor. But most modern Jews do acknowledge his valuable contributions as an historical writer—one whose numerous biases can be identified and filtered out. While living in Roman luxury, Josephus wrote two great histories. One of them, *The Antiquities of the Jews*, written around A.D. 93, traces the Jews from Creation until A.D. 66. It is a fertile source for our knowledge about the Jews, Christians, and Romans in early to mid first-century Palestine. Both Jesus and John the Baptist are described.

For purposes of Christian history, Josephus's most famous passage is his description of Jesus.[9] It appears in all the extant manuscripts and was quoted by Eusebius as early as A.D. 325.[10] But this passage has long been controversial, primarily because (1) it identifies Jesus as "Christ" (the Greek word for the Jewish messiah), and (2) it states as a fact that he appeared to his disciples alive on the third day after his crucifixion. Neither of these statements would likely have been made by a non-Christian, Jewish historian. So some scholars have dismissed the entire passage as a later Christian insertion into the manuscripts of Josephus's book. But this conclusion may be too drastic. Most modern scholars think that Josephus, in his account of Pontius Pilate's governorship of Judea, did indeed include a few sentences about Jesus. It would have been perfectly normal for a Jewish historian to mention Pilate's crucifixion of a rabble-rousing Jewish rabbi during a Passover celebration in Jerusalem. But it would *not* have been normal for him to embellish the record with an acknowledgment that this rabbi was the Messiah and had risen from the dead. So these sorts of

---

[9] Josephus, "The Antiquities of the Jews" 18.63-64, *The Works*, trans. William Whiston, new updtd. ed. (Peabody, MA: Hendrickson, 1987), p. 480.

[10] Eusebius, *The History of the Church* 1.11, trans. G. A. Williamson, rev. ed. (London: Penguin Group, 1989), p. 29.

comments were probably inserted into the manuscripts by some unknown later Christians.

Professor F. F. Bruce pieced together a well-accepted reconstruction of what Josephus most likely wrote about Jesus. It is faithful to the early manuscript text, it eliminates the probable alterations by later Christians, and it is similar to a recently discovered Arabic manuscript written by a tenth-century Melkite (Christian) historian.[11]

> About this time there arose a source of further troubles in one Jesus, a wise man and a wonder-worker. . .He led away many Jews. . .This man was the so-called Christ. When Pilate, acting on information supplied by the chief men among us [Jews], condemned him to the cross, those who had attached themselves to him at the first did not abandon their allegiance, and the tribe of Christians, which has taken this name from him, is not extinct even today.[12]

This kind of statement, written by a prominent Jew about sixty years after the crucifixion, is strong corroborative evidence for the gospel stories of Jesus' existence, ministry, and death.

Josephus wrote one other reference to Jesus. This time there is no reason to doubt that it has come down to us in accurate form. He states that, during the three months it took for a new governor to arrive from Rome after the death of his predecessor (probably in A.D. 62), a new high priest was appointed. This priest was:

> a bold man in his temper, and very insolent; . . .[S]o he assembled the sanhedrin of judges, and brought before them the brother of Jesus, who was called Christ, whose name was James, and some others; and when he had formed an accusation against them as breakers of the law, he delivered them to be stoned.[13]

---

[11] Josephus, *The Essential Writings*, trans. and ed. Paul L. Maier (Grand Rapids, MI: Kregel Publications, 1988), p. 265, n.

[12] F. F. Bruce, *New Testament History*, p. 166.

[13] Josephus, "The Antiquities of the Jews" 20.197-200, *The Works*, pp. 537-538.

This reference confirms that Jesus was indeed considered by some people to be the Messiah. It also confirms Paul's statement that Jesus had a brother named James.[14]

These early non-Christian references to Jesus eliminate the issue of *whether* he was, allowing us to focus instead on *who* he was. To that end, we must now examine the manuscript evidence for the New Testament gospels. Do these ancient Christian documents constitute reliable records of Jesus' birth, life, and death?

---

[14] Galatians 1:19. Matthew and Mark also mention Jesus' brother named James, including him in a list of several other brothers and sisters. Matthew 13:55–56; Mark 6:3. As Mary's firstborn, Jesus would have been older than his siblings.

Chapter Four

✝

MANUSCRIPT EVIDENCE FOR THE GOSPELS

INTRODUCTION

The historical truth of the Christian faith is firmly rooted in the New Testament gospels. These four books describe a wandering Jewish prophet named Jesus. He was born in Bethlehem between 7 and 3 B.C., was circumcised on the eighth day, and sometime later fled with his parents to Egypt to escape King Herod (who ruled over most of Palestine at that time). The family eventually returned to their home in Nazareth, where Jesus was raised and evidently helped his father in the construction/carpentry business. We know nothing about his schooling, but he did visit the temple in Jerusalem at age twelve. Around age thirty he was baptized by John the Baptist, following which he embarked on a three-year ministry of preaching, teaching, healing, and performing miraculous feats. He was crucified in Jerusalem around A.D. 30. Within about forty hours after dying on the cross, he was allegedly resurrected from the dead.

If the bedrock facts described in the Gospels are nothing more than fiction, then Christianity falls on its face—just another philosophical system of ethical behavior on Earth and myths about life after death. But if the gospel claim is true—if this man Jesus was God in the flesh—then Christianity is not mere human speculation about the world around us and about life after death. It is something radically different—something that cannot be sensibly ignored. Therefore, the most reasonable course of action is to examine the Gospels, test them by the same standards used in evaluating any other book that claims to be historically true, and then draw one's own conclusion.

In deciding whether the Gospels are reliable records of various facts about Jesus' life, death, teachings, and claims, three distinct questions need to be considered.

1. Have our modern English New Testaments been accurately translated from the ancient Greek manuscripts?
2. Were those ancient Greek manuscripts copied accurately from the long-lost original gospel documents? This question involves some subsidiary issues. For example, how much time elapsed between the writing of the originals and the production of our oldest existing copies? And how many of the old copies still exist as usable crosschecks against each other for accuracy?
3. Did the original Gospels accurately describe the people, places, and events that they portrayed? This question also involves some subsidiary issues. For example, how much time elapsed between the events themselves and the writing of the original manuscripts? During that time gap, in what oral or written forms were the stories handed down? Could exaggeration and legend have crept in? How much external evidence corroborates our modern reconstructions of the original manuscripts? And do the internal differences among the four Gospels diminish their reliability as accurate records of historical events?

These questions must be explored and answered before any conclusions can be drawn about the Christian claim that Jesus was the Son of God.

This chapter examines the manuscripts. Chapters five and six will analyze the evidence that corroborates them. Chapters seven and eight will then focus on the evidence relating to Christianity's central issue: Was Jesus really resurrected from the dead? If he was, then this remarkable event supplies powerful evidence for his divinity. If not, then Jesus was just another teacher of human ethics and philosopher about life after death—albeit one whose own personal ethics and philosophy would be darkly clouded by his false claim of divinity.

AUTHORSHIP OF THE FOUR GOSPELS

Before turning to the translation and manuscript issues, we need to look briefly at the authorship of the four Gospels. Although the documents themselves are anonymous, Matthew, Mark, Luke, and John have traditionally been considered as the authors. Matthew and John were two of Jesus' disciples; Mark was an early church missionary and probably the disciple Peter's companion in Rome; Luke (who also wrote the book of Acts) was a gentile friend and companion of the apostle Paul.

These traditional authorships continue to be debated. But most likely Mark and Luke did indeed write the Gospels that bear their names. Mark probably recorded Peter's memories, and, if so, his gospel reports an eyewitness account of Jesus' ministry.[1] Moreover, Mark's use of the Greek language reveals Aramaic idioms, meaning that his gospel may reflect the oral Aramaic preaching in the early church.

Luke's probable authorship of the book of Acts buttresses the likelihood that he also wrote its companion volume, the gospel to which his name has been assigned. The author opens this gospel with the statement that *he*:

> carefully investigated everything from the beginning. . .to write an orderly account. . .[2]

We have no good reason to doubt this claim.

The authorships of Matthew and John are more debatable, but each man may well have been involved in writing the gospel that bears his name. Perhaps they each led small groups of followers who helped in the work of putting pen to papyrus, meaning that these two Gospels could have been drafted (or at least edited) by

---

[1] So stated by Papias, Bishop of Hieropolis, around A.D. 130–140, preserved by Eusebius about A.D. 325 in *The History of the Church* 3.39, pp. 103–104. Moreover, in his own first letter from Rome, around A.D. 62, Peter included greetings from Mark (1 Peter 5:13).

[2] Luke 1:3.

committees. We may never know for sure. But John's gospel does point in that direction, stating near the end that:

> this is the disciple who testifies to these things and who wrote them down. *We* know that his testimony is true.[3]

Despite the uncertainties from our own vantage point two thousand years later, church leaders from the early centuries unanimously attributed the two Gospels to Matthew and John. And the earliest documents show that all four Gospels, no matter who wrote them, were universally considered by the churches to be authoritative records of Jesus' life, teachings, death, and resurrection.

The Gospels were written by people who functioned as typical historiographers of their time, i.e., they wrote analyses of selected sources. They did not serve as "biographers" of Jesus, in our modern sense of that word, even though their writings do contain a great deal of biographical information. When compared with Greek historians like Herodotus and Thucydides (from the fifth century B.C.) and the Jewish historian Josephus (from the first century A.D.), the accounts of the gospel authors constitute normal historical writings of that era.

Matthew, Mark, and Luke are commonly called the "synoptic" Gospels, because they share many similarities in structure, language, and content. By contrast, John's gospel stands apart, containing much material that does not appear in the synoptics.

TRANSLATION OF THE NEW TESTAMENT INTO MODERN ENGLISH

The modern English New Testament is derived from about five thousand old Greek manuscripts, many of which have come down to us from as early as the second, third, and fourth centuries A.D. Some of them are complete, while others are only fragmentary. It is from these old manuscripts that modern English translators have gone to work.

---

[3] John 21:24; (emphasis added.)

The languages spoken in Palestine during Jesus' time were primarily Semitic (Aramaic and Hebrew) and Greek. While the Old Testament had been composed in Hebrew, the original New Testament manuscripts were written in Greek. So, in examining the Gospels for historical accuracy, we must look at the path of their translation into modern English.

During the early centuries, handwritten copies of the original Greek language Gospels, along with the other New Testament documents, enjoyed wide circulation. They were often translated into various Middle Eastern languages, including Syriac and Coptic, for use by missionaries. Then, around A.D. 400, a Christian scholar named Jerome produced a translation of the entire Bible into Latin, commonly called the Vulgate. In the sixth century it was brought to England, remaining as that country's primary Bible for several hundred years. A number of partial translations were produced in the emerging English language, but not until 1382 was the first entire English language Bible completed. Named after its prime mover, John Wycliffe, this Bible was translated directly from the Latin. Thus the Wycliffe New Testament was a translation from a translation (Greek to Latin to English).

In 1525 William Tyndale produced the first English translation directly from Greek, using a new text that had been compiled and published just a few years earlier by the humanist scholar Erasmus of Rotterdam. In effect, Tyndale opened the floodgates. During the rest of the sixteenth century, many new English translations were produced, culminating in the King James Version of 1611 (often called the Authorized Version). It remained the standard English version of the Bible until newer and more modern translations began to appear around the beginning of the twentieth century.

The King James Version was produced by some fifty scholars, commissioned by the King. The title page bears the statement that they had translated from the original languages (Hebrew for the Old Testament and Greek for the New Testament) and had diligently compared and revised the previous English translations. During the next century and a half, their 1611 text underwent several revisions.

Without doubt, the King James scholars produced an extraordinary and enduring work—one that is still favored by many people for its majestic and poetic language. But Elizabethan English is no longer in use, thus rendering the King James Version difficult to read and sometimes hard to understand. Moreover, Erasmus's Greek text, on which the scholars based their translation, was itself derived from manuscripts dating back no further than the tenth century A.D. This created a problem of accuracy, because in the centuries *after* the King James Version was produced many more Greek New Testament manuscripts were discovered. They were earlier and more reliable than the manuscripts that had been available to the King James scholars. Furthermore, archaeologists had discovered hundreds of ordinary, non-literary documents written in everyday (as distinct from classical) Greek. This was the very language in which the New Testament had first been written. But no examples of this everyday language had been accessible to the King James translators. As a result, the twentieth century has produced many new English translations and paraphrases of the original Greek texts that are more accurate than the King James Version could possibly have been.

But translation from Greek into English is not the only step that must be accounted for. The original gospel authors themselves probably had to translate Jesus' oral statements from a picturesque and uncomplicated Semitic language (Aramaic or Hebrew) into the precise and delicate written form of a complex Indo-European language (Greek). This translation into Greek may have taken place even before the Gospels were first written—at a time when the stories of Jesus and his teachings were being preserved in oral form or as informal written notes. If that was the case, then the many linguistic similarities between the three synoptic Gospels would be easier to explain than if Matthew, Mark, and Luke had each produced his own individual translation from Aramaic into Greek. Even though we are unlikely to ever know the details, the important fact is that eighteen or nineteen centuries later these ancient Greek texts have been converted into modern English.

The translation process is far more difficult than most of us realize. Words, phrases, and nuances in one language may not have exact equivalents in another. And the translator will always be faced with threshold decisions, such as whether to seek a word-for-word equivalence or a meaning-for-meaning equivalence. If an ancient document contains many metaphors and idioms, a word-for-word translation will inevitably lose some of the flavor that the author intended to impart. But a meaning-for-meaning translation, using the sentence—not the individual word—as the unit of translation, creates the risk that the translator will be too subjective in selecting modern words and phrases to reproduce an ancient author's underlying meaning.

The complexity of the translation process can be illustrated by situations in which a particular Greek word has multiple meanings. A good example is Luke's famous Christmas story about how Jesus was born in a Bethlehem stable because there was no room for Mary and Joseph at the inn.[4] In fact, there probably was no such "inn." Nor was there a hard-hearted innkeeper who guided them to a stable out back, forcing Jesus to be born in a lowly manger (an animal feeding trough). The problem is one of translation. The English word "inn" appears in Luke's story as the Greek word *kataluma*, a general word for "lodging place." Technically, it could be used for a commercial inn, but some scholars have recently realized that this is not what Luke likely meant. Why not? Because later in his gospel Luke tells us that Jesus and his disciples took their Last Supper in a *kataluma*,[5] which Luke specifically describes as a large, furnished guest room on the upper floor of a private home. It doesn't make much sense to assume that Luke used the same Greek word to mean one thing in his story of the Last Supper and something quite different in his account of Jesus' birth.

This conclusion is strengthened by the fact that Luke was well aware of the normal Greek word for a commercial inn. In his account of Jesus' parable about the Good Samaritan, Luke says that the Samaritan took the wounded man to a *pandocheion*.[6] This is

---

[4] Luke 2:4–7.

[5] Luke 22:11–12.

[6] Luke 10:34–35.

the specific Greek word for a *public* lodging place, i.e., an "inn." If Luke had meant to tell us that Jesus' birth took place behind an inn, why didn't he use the same specific word that he employed in the parable of the Good Samaritan, rather than the general word he used for the upper room of the Last Supper? The answer seems clear enough. He was not reporting that Jesus was born behind an inn. Instead, he was probably telling us this: When Joseph and Mary arrived in Bethlehem for the Roman census, the guest room of the private home in which they had planned to stay was already being occupied by other people who were also in town for the census. So Mary, Joseph, and the homeowners probably shared the house's single living room, and the birth was accomplished right there. Jesus was laid in the safest and cleanest place available—the straw-filled manger at the far end of the floor. It was right next to the lowered part of the room where the animals were housed at night, as was customary in the one- and two-room Palestinian houses of that era. The net result is that today's charming Christmas stories and pageants probably paint a somewhat erroneous picture of what really happened two thousand years ago—all because a single Greek word appears to have been inaccurately translated.

Another example of translation difficulties is contained in one of Paul's statements. The *New Revised Standard Version* of the Bible translates verse 8:28 of his letter to the Romans as:

> *all things* work together for good for those who love God (emphasis added).

This means that the "things" themselves, as the subjects of the sentence, do the actual working for good. By contrast, the *New International Version* translates this passage as:

> in all things *God* works for the good of those who love him (emphasis added).

This translation means that God, as the subject of the sentence, does the actual working for good (within the context of whatever the "things" happen to be).

The difference in meaning between the two versions is significant. To illustrate, if an infant is killed by a drunken driver, the NRSV translation states that the event itself will work for the good of the grieving, God-loving parents. Frankly, that just doesn't ring true for many people. But the NIV translation states that, in the aftermath of the awful event, God—not the event—will work to bring some good to those parents. For most people, this is a more comforting concept. The point of the illustration is not that one translation is more accurate than the other. Rather, the point is that the original Greek sentence is not entirely clear. So an "accurate" translation into English simply cannot be guaranteed.

To summarize, translation is a complicated process, often involving a certain amount of interpretation. The goal of reproducing an ancient author's precise meaning is not always easy, or even possible, to achieve.

EXISTING GREEK MANUSCRIPT COPIES OF THE GOSPELS

The New Testament, as we know it today, and as it has existed since ancient times, consists of the four Gospels and twenty-three other documents. The entire collection is typically referred to as a set of "books," but in reality that term only applies to the four Gospels and the book of Acts. The other twenty-two documents are actually letters, most of them having been written by the apostle Paul.

Where can the oldest existing manuscripts of these twenty-seven documents be found today?

The search might best begin with the first great parchment manuscripts of the Greek New Testament, produced around A.D. 350. Only two of them have come down to us: the Codex Sinaiticus,[7] found in 1859 at Saint Catherine's Monastery on the Sinai Peninsula and now displayed in London's British Museum, and the Codex Vaticanus, now part of the Vatican Library in

---

[7] The word *codex* means a manuscript written on pages that were assembled into a volume, as distinct from a manuscript written on a single long scroll that had to be rolled up from the ends.

Rome. Both codices are descendants of the great scriptorium at Alexandria (a sort of ancient publishing house on the Mediterranean coast of Egypt). This city was a scholarly center and the home of a celebrated ancient library. Beginning in the second century A.D., the scribes at Alexandria's scriptorium strove to produce New Testament texts that were free from the copying errors which had already begun to creep into earlier manuscripts. Their work became a model for smaller scriptoriums in rural areas of Egypt. To this day, the Alexandrian text, along with the Western and Byzantine families of texts,[8] is a primary source for reconstructing the original New Testament documents.

Ancient historical documents like Sinaiticus and Vaticanus, produced within about 320 years after the reported events, are entitled to considerable evidentiary weight as reliable sources for the original text. This is especially true when they are compared with the oldest existing records of other events from the same general era. For example, as evidence for what happened during Julius Caesar's campaign in ancient Gaul, only nine or ten good manuscript copies of his *Gallic War* still exist. The oldest one was produced more than 900 years after the events. We do not know what happened to the original manuscripts or to any copies of them that may have been made in the early centuries. Similarly, the Greek historian Thucydides wrote his *History* in the fifth century B.C., but we know about it from only eight manuscript copies, the earliest of which was produced more than 1,300 years after the original had been written.

---

[8] At the same time the Alexandrian text was being developed (second and third centuries A.D.), another, and somewhat less trustworthy group of texts, was also being produced. It came to be called the Western text. Then, after the persecution by the Roman Emperor Diocletian in A.D. 303, a smooth, well-edited, and independent type of text was composed. Based upon manuscripts of varying quality, and introducing many textual changes, it became the standard text for the Eastern Church and the source of the text that is known as Byzantine. After Latin became the dominant language around the Mediterranean, the Greek-speaking churches of the east were the only ones that continued to make copies of the Greek text. Thus, for many centuries most New Testament manuscripts were produced in the Byzantine text.

Not only the age, but also the very completeness of the New Testament manuscripts is important, especially when compared with the fragmentary nature of other ancient manuscripts. For instance, Livy's *History of Rome*, written just before Jesus' time, originally consisted of 142 books. But only thirty-five of them have come down to us today, the oldest copy dating no further back than the fourth century A.D. The rest—107 books out of the original 142—were lost. Likewise, much of the work of the Roman historian Tacitus, written shortly after A.D. 100, has been lost. We know his *Histories* only from the four and a half surviving books and his *Annals* from the twelve that remain out of the original sixteen. And our knowledge of all these surviving books comes from only two medieval manuscript copies, one dated to the ninth century A.D. and the other to the eleventh.

By comparison with these ancient secular writings, the evidence of the Codex Sinaiticus and Codex Vaticanus is quite powerful. A time gap of about 320 years between the events themselves and these old parchment manuscripts gives us significant comfort that they are accurate records. But the comfort level would be even higher if the manuscript evidence were earlier and more abundant. Fortunately, older and more extensive New Testament manuscripts do exist. They were written on papyrus.

This ancient form of paper, made from an aquatic, grasslike plant, was not as durable as the parchment (produced from animal skins) that came into extensive use during the third and fourth centuries A.D. Among the existing papyrus manuscripts of the New Testament, some are nearly complete. Others are only portions of a page. But, collectively, these old papyrus manuscripts provide us with many copies of the entire Greek New Testament. As a result, the task of converting them into modern English should have been a straightforward matter of translation. But it was not quite that simple.

Naturally, all the papyrus manuscript copies were made by hand (mostly from earlier copies). So the potential for scribal errors was significant, and the resulting variations among the copies complicate the task of reconstructing the original New Testament texts.

But the complicated cloud has a silver lining: The very abundance of diverse papyrus manuscripts provides a vast self-correcting mechanism. No other ancient text possesses such a wealth of early and abundant manuscript evidence. Scholars and students of ancient classical works (and even of the Old Testament) have a right to be jealous of the attestation that is available for the New Testament. Using this extensive array of manuscripts, scholars can reconstruct, with a high degree of confidence, the original Greek gospel texts, just as they came from the pens of the authors.

Most of the scribal differences among the various manuscripts of a single gospel are minor matters of spelling, grammar, and the like. But not all of them can be so labeled. Substantive variations do indeed exist among the collection of manuscripts for each particular gospel. For example, the last twelve verses in Mark's gospel[9] do not appear in any of the earliest and best manuscripts. They were evidently added at some unknown later date, perhaps because the last page or two had been lost from the original.[10] Another example of a significant variation is the story in John's gospel about the woman caught in adultery. To her accusers Jesus said, "If any one of you is without sin, let him be the first to throw a stone at her."[11] This anecdote does not appear in any of the earliest manuscripts. It was probably a true story from the early traditions about Jesus that did not find its way into one of the original gospel accounts.[12]

Other examples of episodes that are not present in the earliest manuscripts of a gospel are Luke's statement that, while Jesus was praying in the Garden of Gethsemane, his "sweat was like drops of

---

[9] Mark 16:9–20.

[10] It probably could not have happened this way if the writing had been done on a traditional Jewish scroll. However, the original gospels were among the first ancient documents to be produced in the form of individual pages bound together like a book.

[11] John 7:53–8:11.

[12] Philip Wesley Comfort, *The Quest for the Original Text of the New Testament* (Grand Rapids, MI: Baker Book House, 1992), pp. 144–145.

blood,"[13] and Luke's description of Jesus' prayer from the cross, "Father, forgive them, for they do not know what they are doing."[14] Once again, these could well be true stories (from early oral traditions) that were omitted from the original Gospels. We may never know for sure. But the omission of such stories from the earliest manuscripts should not corrode our confidence. The thousands of surviving Greek manuscripts furnish a trustworthy source for accurately reconstructing the text of the original Gospels. No fundamental Christian doctrine rests on any of the relatively few uncertain passages.

Among all the papyrus manuscript copies, the earlier ones ought normally to be the best sources from which to reconstruct the original gospel texts. If so, where did they come from, and how old are they?

During the past hundred years, archaeologists have discovered many of them in the dry sands of middle Egypt. Some were written as early as the second century A.D. Until recently, the oldest one appeared to be a piece of papyrus containing several verses from the Gospel of John.[15] It confirms the language appearing in later Greek manuscript copies of the Gospel. This fragment, now kept in the Rylands Library at Manchester, England, is paleographically dated to about A.D. 120—less than a hundred years after Jesus' crucifixion. That is a very short time gap by ancient standards.

But an even earlier date for a gospel manuscript copy has recently been claimed—and then promptly disputed by most scholars. The claim was put forward by a German scholar, who announced his paleographic conclusion that three fragments of Matthew's gospel had probably been produced in the A.D. 60s—

---

[13] Luke 22:44; Philip Wesley Comfort, *The Quest for the Original Text of the New Testament*, pp. 141–142.

[14] Luke 23:34; Philip Wesley Comfort, *The Quest for the Original Text of the New Testament*, p. 142.

[15] John 18:31–33, 37–38.

only thirty or forty years after Jesus' crucifixion.[16] These fragments have been in the custody of Oxford's Magdalen College since 1901, when they were acquired from one of the college's graduates working in Luxor, Egypt. A few years later the graduate was killed in a Sicilian earthquake, and most of his papers and notes were lost in the rubble. So nothing is known about the original source of the three fragments.

The Rylands fragment, and possibly the three Magdalen fragments, along with many other early papyrus manuscript copies, provides powerful evidence for the accuracy of the later parchment manuscripts. But before checking the dates of some of these other papyrus manuscripts, we should briefly set the stage by determining why they were buried beneath Egyptian sands in the first place.

Immediately after the original gospel manuscripts were written (between about A.D. 60 and 90, as will be shown later in this chapter), copies were needed by local churches and missionaries so that the authoritative story of Jesus could be read aloud to largely illiterate audiences. Some of the copies were professionally produced in large scriptoriums. Others were made in small scriptoriums (or by individual Christians) at local churches. The quality of these handwritten papyrus copies varied from place to place. If only one or two of them had survived to the present day, we could have relatively little confidence in their accuracy as copies of the originals. But, as noted above, a large number did survive. Thus the confidence level can be quite high.

There is no way of knowing how many old copies were actually produced during the first hundred years or so after the originals had been penned. The uncertainty stems from the Roman emperor Diocletian's widespread persecution of Christians in A.D. 303. It was most severe in Palestine, Egypt, and North Africa. Al-

---

[16] Carsten Peter Thiede, and Matthew D'Ancona, *Eyewitness to Jesus* (New York: Doubleday, 1996). The authors also point out that a tiny papyrus fragment deposited in Qumran Cave 7 sometime prior to A.D. 68 is probably from an early copy of Mark's gospel.

though not the earliest persecution of Christians, it was the first one that included destruction of their sacred documents. The only writings that appear to have escaped destruction were those which had been hidden away. Among them, about forty full or partial manuscripts are known to have survived to the present time. None was discovered near Alexandria, with its great library and scriptorium, because if any had been hidden there the papyrus would have long since rotted away in the dampness and high water table of the Mediterranean coast. In fact, only if a manuscript were hidden in a place like the hot, dry sands of middle and upper Egypt, far south of the coast, would it have had a chance for long-term preservation. And it is precisely in those southern sands where the surviving, pre- A.D. 303, papyrus manuscripts were discovered.

Oxyrhynchus, two hundred miles south of the Mediterranean and ten miles west of the Nile, was an old city in rural Egypt. It was probably an intellectual center for Christianity, with ties to the Alexandria scriptorium. From 1897 to 1907, in an Oxyrhynchus rubbish heap, a treasure-trove of everyday ancient documents was uncovered—letters, legal papers, and business records, as well as some classical literary works and Christian commentaries. Also uncovered were thirty-six partial New Testament papyrus manuscripts. Most of them had been produced between A.D. 200 and 400, and a few were dated even earlier. They had become worn from use by early Christians and were evidently discarded after being replaced by new copies. The A.D. 120 fragment of John's gospel, noted above, probably came from Oxyrhynchus. Acquired in Egypt in 1917, it strongly suggests that the gospel was originally composed before A.D. 100.[17] And it flatly disproves skeptical scholarly opinion, voiced in the late nineteenth century, that John's gospel had not been written until around A.D. 200.

Another discovery of New Testament documents in Egypt was announced by the *London Times* in 1931. Twelve manuscripts had been found in jars in a Coptic graveyard and were subsequently

---

[17] F. F. Bruce, *The New Testament Documents*, pp. 17–18; Philip Wesley Comfort, *The Quest for the Original Text of the New Testament*, pp. 31, 64.

purchased from a Cairo dealer. The alleged discovery site was probably incorrectly identified by the Egyptian excavators so as to conceal the precise location of their discovery. But quite possibly the manuscripts came from an Egyptian church, where they were hidden during the Diocletian persecution. Copies of three New Testament codices were included: the four Gospels and Acts, produced between A.D. 150 and 200; Paul's letters, produced between A.D. 85 and 200; and the book of Revelation, produced between A.D. 200 and 300.

A third major discovery occurred in 1952, when an assortment of old manuscripts was uncovered near the Dishna Plain in Egypt, about two hundred miles southeast of Oxyrhynchus and fifty miles north of Thebes. It consisted of literary works, like Homer's *Iliad* and *Odyssey* and Thucydides's *History*, as well as various Greek and Coptic Christian writings. It also included some Greek New Testament manuscripts. One of them was a Gospel of John, probably produced between A.D. 150 and 175 (although the director of Papyrological Collections at the National Library in Vienna dated it as early as A.D. 125). Another manuscript contained most of Luke's and John's Gospels. Dated to about A.D. 175, it is considered the best extant copy of any substantial portion of the New Testament, having been elegantly and accurately produced, probably by a professional copyist in Alexandria. All the Dishna documents likely came from a monastery library, which contained some poor quality copies (perhaps made by the local monks) and some excellent copies (perhaps produced at a scriptorium like Alexandria's).

Today these various New Testament papyrus manuscripts, scattered far from where they were discovered, are housed at places like the Beatty Museum near Dublin, the University of Michigan library, the Rylands Library at Manchester, and the Bodmer Library of World Literature near Geneva.

All of this leads to two inescapable conclusions. First, the New Testament is supported by a greater number of early papyrus copies than any other ancient history book. They provide an extensive mechanism for comparing copies against each other in order to accurately reconstruct the original texts. Second, the existing papyrus copies of the New Testament were written much sooner after the original manuscripts, and much closer to the recorded events themselves, than is the case for any other ancient history book. So it can no longer be seriously claimed that the New Testament is tainted by editorial revisions from later generations of Christian theologians.

Skeptics ought to acknowledge right up front that attestation of the New Testament manuscripts far surpasses the substantiation of any other ancient historical work. Then they will be free to examine the underlying factual content of the New Testament manuscripts for errors, biases, and exaggerations. To the extent that none can be found, those manuscripts will be entitled to the face value presumption of historical accuracy.

ORIGINAL GOSPEL MANUSCRIPTS

We now need to look at the time period within which the four Gospels were originally composed. The job is not simple, because all the originals have long since been lost. Nevertheless, time frames are important. A long time gap between the actual events of Jesus' life and the first written accounts would diminish gospel credibility. As ancient decades rolled by, legend and exaggeration would more likely have slipped into the record. By contrast, a short time gap would enhance the credibility of the accounts, since legends and exaggerations do not spring full-blown onto the pages of history. They need a period of time to develop before finding their way into written records. Moreover, if the time gap was short, eyewitnesses would still be around to dispute any misstatements.

And eyewitnesses would not be the only ones. Members of Jesus' own family were available. A second-century Jewish Christian writer, Hegesippus, relates that the emperor Domitian, who reigned from A.D. 81 to 96, had ordered that the members of King David's line be executed. Accordingly, the grandsons of Jude, the brother of Jesus, were brought before the emperor. They admitted their lineage, but emphasized that they were only poor laborers.

Finding no fault with them, Domitian let them go free.[18] This story reveals that members of Jesus' family lived into later decades and would have been on hand to dispute any misstatements in written accounts of their great uncle's life and work and death.

So dating the original gospel manuscripts is a cornerstone of any effort to assess their historical accuracy. But, at best, it is an exercise in educated speculation. The most that any scholar can hope for is to draw some rational conclusions from some fairly meager evidence.

During the nineteenth century, many scholars dated the original Gospels and other New Testament documents to sometime between A.D. 150 and 200. This allowed them to argue that plenty of time had elapsed for legend and exaggeration to permeate the stories about Jesus. But, from the very outset, their "late-dating" theory was on shaky conceptual ground. By A.D. 200, the Christian church had long since shed its Jewish roots and become a gentile movement. So the nineteenth-century scholars necessarily assumed that *gentile* authors of the late second century A.D. could have devised the Gospels' accurate and comprehensive description of a *Jewish* culture that had vanished more than a century earlier. This was, at the very least, a dubious assumption. But the real disintegration of the "late-dating" theory commenced when the ancient Greek papyrus manuscripts began to emerge from Egyptian sands at the end of the nineteenth century. The scholars who combed these manuscripts were compelled to start all over in developing probable dates for the original Gospels.

The consensus has long been that Jesus was crucified sometime around A.D. 30. Thus the original Gospels could not have been written before that date. Extant *copies* of the originals—copies that can be touched, viewed, and studied today—were being produced in the second century, at least as early as A.D. 120. This gives us a window of about ninety years between the events of Jesus' life and the earliest existing copy of a gospel. Working within that window, most scholars now agree that all the original gospel

---

[18] Preserved by Eusebius, *The History of the Church* 3.19–20, pp. 81–82.

documents were written between about A.D. 60 and 90. So skeptics don't have very many years at their disposal in arguing that legend and exaggeration infiltrated the accounts.

Modern scholars do not know for certain whether the four gospel authors worked independently of one another, or whether they collaborated closely and borrowed extensively from each other, or whether the truth lies somewhere in between. The theories vary widely, and, to some extent, they influence the issue of dating. For example, many scholars think that Mark's gospel was the first to be composed. Most of them also think it was then used as source material by Matthew and Luke, who both added elements from another (but unknown) source.[19] Other scholars take a different view, agreeing with early church leaders who were satisfied that Matthew's gospel was the first to be written. A few scholars think that each synoptic gospel author used an entirely independent tradition in compiling his account. Complicating the situation is the fact that scholars also disagree about the extent to which the gospel writers merely compiled their accounts from material that already existed, as distinct from using their own editorial research and judgment.

And so the debate plods along. We will probably never have definitive answers. But, in the meantime, we do have some specific evidence and some logical arguments that support a relatively early dating for the original gospels.

1. We possess today a record of various documents written by early Christian leaders during the Church's formative period. Some of these men died as martyrs, while others lived a full life span. Many of their writings refer to New Testament texts, thus providing evidence that those texts had been written and were being circulated by the time the particular church leader wrote his own document. One prominent example is Clement, a leader of the Roman church. Writing to the church at Corinth by about

---

[19] F. F. Bruce, *The New Testament Documents*, pp. 33–35.

A.D. 96 or 97, he referred to various texts, including material that is part of the Gospels and other New Testament books. He even used the word *gospel* in describing what the apostles had received from Jesus, and he quotes words of Jesus that are the same as Jesus' words recorded in the Gospels of Matthew and Luke. Similarly, Ignatius, Bishop of Antioch, wrote letters to various churches while he was on his way to Roman martyrdom in A.D. 117. In the letter to Smyrna (modern Izmir, on the west coast of Turkey), he quotes the resurrected Jesus' invitation for a doubting Thomas to physically touch his hands. Virtually the same language appears in Luke's gospel. Another example is Polycarp, Bishop of Smyrna. Around A.D. 110, he wrote a letter to the church at Philippi (an ancient city in modern Greece, near the north shore of the Aegean Sea). In the letter, he quotes extensively from New Testament writings, including John's first epistle, which was probably a covering letter for John's gospel. Like Clement, he quotes words of Jesus just as they appear in the Gospels of Matthew and Luke.

Thus, from the writings of these three early church leaders, we know that certain gospel (and other New Testament) texts were in existence, were in circulation, and were being referred to, all within about sixty-five to eighty-five years after the actual historical events had occurred.

2. The city of Jerusalem, along with its famous temple, was destroyed by the Romans in A.D. 70. Yet none of the gospel accounts contains even a hint that this Jewish tragedy had already occurred. Admittedly, the gospel authors, three of whom were Jews,[20] may have had reasons for remaining silent about the matter. And arguments from silence certainly deserve a degree of skepticism. But it is still curious that some sort of oblique reference to the historical fact of Jerusalem's destruction did not sneak into one of their accounts. This is

---

[20] Matthew, Mark, and John. Luke was a Gentile.

especially true of Matthew, who, writing his gospel for a Jewish audience, even commented about payment of the temple tax.[21] This would have been an odd subject to mention after A.D. 70, when the temple no longer existed and when all of its tax revenues were being sent to the pagan temple of Jupiter in Rome. Along this line, a British scholar used the destruction of Jerusalem and its temple as an important factor in his thesis that all four Gospels were originally written before A.D. 70.[22]

3. Luke's book of Acts, a companion volume to his gospel, ends abruptly with Paul's Roman imprisonment, which we know from various sources took place in the early A.D. 60s. Yet the book of Acts contains no mention of Paul's subsequent beheading, which occurred in the mid- A.D. 60s. Nor does it allude to the martyrdoms of Peter and of James (the brother of Jesus), which also took place in the A.D. 60s. These omissions are quite unusual, considering the fact that Luke specifically describes the earlier martyrdoms of Stephen and of James (the brother of John).[23] Once again, we are faced with an argument from silence. But, if the martyrdoms of three prominent Christian leaders (Paul, Peter, and James) had taken place before Acts was written, it is certainly plausible to think that Luke would have mentioned at least one of them, just as he mentioned the two earlier martyrdoms of Stephen and James. Assuming, then, that Acts was indeed written in the 60s, Luke's gospel must have been written even earlier, because his book of Acts opens with a specific reference to:

my former book. . .about all that Jesus began to do and to teach until the day he was taken up to heaven.[24]

---

[21] Matthew 17:24–27.

[22] J. A. T. Robinson, *Redating the New Testament* (London: SCM Press, 1976).

[23] Acts 7:54–60; 12:2.

[24] Acts 1:1–2 (emphasis added).

4. The apostle Paul, writing between A.D. 48 and the mid-60s, sent
    a number of letters to various Christian churches and
    individuals. In the letters, he made several purportedly factual
    statements about Jesus, all of which were more fully described
    in the Gospels a few years later: Jesus was a flesh-and-blood
    person who descended from King David and had a brother
    named James; he preached a message; he shared a last supper
    with his disciples; he testified before Pilate; he died by cruci-
    fixion and was buried; he was resurrected on the third day and
    appeared to many of his disciples thereafter.[25] From these early
    Pauline letters we can be sure that this essential information
    about Jesus was well known by at least A.D. 60, thus providing
    even less time for legend or exaggeration to have filtered into
    the original Gospels. We also know that by about A.D. 64, in his
    first letter to Timothy, Paul quoted a passage in Luke's gospel,
    calling it "scripture."[26] All these factors indicate that Luke had
    written his gospel by the early A.D. 60s.

As a result of the evidence, and recognizing that all four Gospels may have been written before Jerusalem's destruction in A.D.
70, the consensus of mainstream scholarly opinion is as follows:
Mark's gospel was written in Rome between A.D. 60 and 70.
Matthew's gospel was written in Syria or Palestine between A.D. 60
and 85. Luke's gospel was written (probably in Rome, but perhaps
in modern Greece or Turkey) between A.D. 60 and 85. And John's
gospel was published (probably in Ephesus, on the west coast of
modern Turkey) by around A.D. 90, although it was perhaps written somewhat earlier. If these dates are approximately correct, then
the maximum time gap between the historical events and the first
written record is about forty years for Mark, about fifty-five years
for Matthew and Luke, and about sixty years for John. These com-
pare favorably with the time gaps for most of the events described

---

[25] Romans 1:3–4 and 10:9; 1 Corinthians 11:23–26 and 15:3–8; Galatians 1:19;
Philippians 2:8; 1 Timothy 3:16 and 6:13; 2 Timothy 2:8.
[26] 1 Timothy 5:18; Luke 10:7.

by the Roman historians Tacitus (forty to ninety years for his Annals) and Suetonius (sixty to one hundred-fifty years).

The short time gap between the gospel events and the original gospel records strengthens the face value presumption of gospel accuracy. The authors are entitled to this presumption no less than other ancient writers of historical events. If modern historians do not seriously question the late and skimpy secular manuscript evidence for writers like Julius Caesar and Cornelius Tacitus, why should anyone devoutly mistrust the early and abundant gospel manuscript evidence for writers like Matthew, Mark, Luke, and John? "Because," someone might reply, "the New Testament deals with a religious subject and must therefore be held to a higher standard." But that's just not good enough. While an author's basic bias can cast doubt on the truth of particular statements, it is an inadequate excuse for rejecting his entire work out of hand.

So the whole historical fabric of the Gospels is entitled to be taken at face value unless there is good reason to dispute certain particular statements. This presumption is especially strong because (as will be seen in ensuing chapters) many factual statements in the Gospels have been confirmed by independent, external evidence. Under these circumstances, the burden of proof falls squarely on the shoulders of skeptics who assert that the gospel authors are biased and cannot be trusted.

SOURCES THAT UNDERLIE THE ORIGINAL GOSPELS

A time gap of less than sixty years between an ancient event and its first written record is not very great. Nevertheless, virtually all scholars agree that the gospel writers used some sort of source material when they first wrote down their accounts. Skeptics can legitimately ask about those sources. Did the authors interview eyewitnesses? Did they have access to written stories about Jesus? Did anybody take contemporaneous notes when Jesus spoke? These kinds of questions deserve the best answers that modern scholarship can provide. But the evidence is admittedly slim.

In the early years after Jesus' crucifixion, the claims about his life, death, resurrection, and deity were undoubtedly proclaimed orally by people who were eyewitnesses, or who had access to eyewitnesses.[27] Fabrication or alteration of their accounts would have created a serious risk of immediate exposure by other eyewitnesses. There was little need for written accounts, particularly in a society with deeply embedded oral tradition. However, as the eyewitnesses grew older the need to preserve their recollections grew stronger. At some early date, compilations of Jesus' teachings must have been written down and assembled. The collections may even have incorporated written notes made by people who were actually present when he taught.

The existence of such compilations can be inferred from the fact that most of the material appearing in Matthew and Luke, but missing from Mark, consists of Jesus' sayings. Thus many scholars have concluded that Matthew and Luke, unlike Mark, probably relied on separate written collections of these sayings. Hints of such collections appear in the second-century writings of early church leaders. For example, Papias, Bishop of Hieropolis around A.D. 130–140, states that:

> Matthew compiled the *Sayings* [of Jesus] in the Aramaic language, and everyone translated them as well as he could.[28]

Moreover, Luke opens his gospel by acknowledging that:

> many have undertaken to draw up an account of the things [about Jesus]. . ., just as they were handed down to us by those who from the first were eyewitnesses.[29]

So from the very early days of the Christian church, stories about Jesus and his sayings had probably been compiled. Some of

[27] An example is Peter's speech at Pentecost, described in Acts 2:14–36.
[28] Eusebius, *The History of the Church* 3.39, trans. G. A. Williamson, rev. ed. (London: Penguin Group, 1989), p. 104. Reproduced by permission of Penguin Books, Ltd.
[29] Luke 1:1–2.

these compilations were likely used in the preparation of Matthew's and Luke's gospels. Even Mark may have utilized them, although his gospel, which reflects the earliest Christian preaching, emphasized Jesus' actions and deeds as the primary way to convert people.

If the collections of Jesus' sayings actually existed, they were probably compiled by A.D. 50, about the same time that Paul was beginning to write his letters and that James (who likely was Jesus' brother) was probably writing the little New Testament book that bears his name. Both Paul and James were certainly familiar with the oral traditions, and quite possibly with the written collections. Thus the documentary roots of the Gospels may well go back to within twenty years of Jesus' crucifixion.

Nevertheless, the story of Jesus must have been first preserved by oral transmission, which was virtually an art form in ancient Middle Eastern culture. Jesus' followers, as Jewish members of that culture, undoubtedly participated in oral transmission and were comfortable with the process. They would surely have had the ability to orally preserve accurate accounts of Jesus' life, although many of the variations among the four Gospels can doubtless be attributed to slight differences between these oral accounts.[30]

Unlike our modern Western attitude that oral transmission is a bit too fluid for comfort, ancient Middle Eastern societies used it as the normal way of passing history from one generation to the next.[31] This pattern persisted in pockets of traditional society throughout the Middle East right up to the advent of television in the mid-twentieth century.

Oral transmission typically occurred during evening gatherings of a group, when people expected to hear and to recite the community's historical recollections and inherited wisdom. The atmosphere was informal, and the group itself identified the best person to tell each particular story. The recited material sometimes took the fixed form of proverbs or poetry. But more often it

---

[30] In addition, as noted earlier, some variations can also be attributed to differing translations of Jesus' Aramaic words into the Greek of the gospels.

[31] Kenneth E. Bailey, "Middle Eastern Oral Tradition and the Synoptic Gospels," *The Expository Times* (September 1995, Vol. 106, No. 12), pp. 363–367.

consisted of stories about the people and events that formed the fabric of the community's identity. In reciting these historical stories, a speaker was allowed some flexibility in stating the essential elements and themes. Of course, the group already knew the material that the speaker was publicly reciting. As a result, the group exercised genuine control over his accuracy and thereby imposed severe limits on his flexibility. Any statements outside those limits would have triggered rejection by the entire community. As a result, Middle Eastern oral tradition was likely to be more reliable than a written historical journal, whose author was not subject to such instant correction by his peers.

The synoptic Gospels contain the very kind of material that was typically handed down by oral transmission: parables and historical stories which traditional village communities recited at their gatherings. So the original Gospels were simply a written product of normal Middle Eastern village life that has existed for thousands of years. Thus, during the brief period in which the gospel accounts were being preserved by oral transmission, they remained reliable. The variations among them were carefully kept within narrow boundaries. Professor Kenneth Bailey capsulized the matter well when he wrote that:

> *designated reciters* of the [Christian] tradition passed their recollections on to the evangelists who then assembled the Gospels.[32]

Skeptics, of course, can argue that thirty to sixty years of oral transmission is long enough for memories to fade. But that's not an adequate response in the context of ancient Middle Eastern culture, where memories were well trained. In fact, studies have even revealed modern examples of traditional African and east European communities in which oral history and folk tales are still being meticulously preserved. The themes and details remain

---

[32] Kenneth E. Bailey, "Middle Eastern Oral Tradition and the Synoptic Gospels," p. 367 (emphasis added).

intact as the stories are passed on, even though the exact wording varies slightly.[33] This is quite similar to what we find in the variations among the New Testament gospels.

Beyond the anthropological studies, we have our own recent example of how memories can readily recall important events and details that happened many years earlier. On June 6, 1994, many people watched televised celebrations of the fiftieth anniversary of World War II's D-Day, when Allied forces invaded Normandy. During the anniversary festivities scores of veterans displayed incredibly detailed recollections of events that had happened fifty years earlier. Those events had been burned into the memory bank of nearly every person who participated in the invasion. Why should anyone think that the people who followed and observed Jesus—the most influential person in their lives—had less reliable memories than those veterans of the 1944 invasion? There is no credible reason for thinking so. On the contrary, we have good grounds to accept at face value the oral eyewitness evidence that underlies the gospel accounts of Jesus.

It must be admitted that, during the early period of oral transmission, a few stories about Jesus seem to have floated around without finding their way into the original Gospels. For example, as noted earlier, the story of the woman caught in adultery[34] is not contained in any of the early Greek manuscripts. So it surely did not appear in the original Gospels. Our first record of the story is from the Syriac Vulgate, which was written early in the fifth century and soon became the standard version of the Syriac church's New Testament. Some decades later the story was included in a fifth/sixth-century Greek manuscript, and also in several subsequent Greek manuscripts. The scribes sometimes inserted it in John's gospel and other times in Luke's (where it was more appropriately positioned). The fact that this story is missing from the early Greek manuscripts is not a serious concern. Its inclusion in the standard Syriac gospel is evidence that it was an accepted story

---

[33] Craig L. Blomberg, *The Historical Reliability of the Gospels*, pp. 28–30.
[34] John 7:53–8:11.

by the Christians in Syria and Mesopotamia (northeast of Palestine) during the centuries after the crucifixion.

When all the scholarly details have been presented and debated, one clear conclusion stands above the fray: Eyewitnesses to Jesus' ministry lingered on for several decades. Their presence would have inhibited any alteration of the truth. And by the time the last eyewitness died, the four Gospels had already been written and were beginning their two-thousand-year journey, through copies and translations, straight into the fabric of our modern society.

FACTUAL DIFFERENCES AMONG THE GOSPEL ACCOUNTS

Readers of the New Testament encounter many factual differences among the four gospel accounts of Jesus' ministry. Thomas Paine paraded them across the pages of his *Age of Reason* as evidence to discredit Christianity, and for many years Paine's book was a major factor in my own religious skepticism. Since then, however, I have come to realize that (putting aside the Gospel of John for separate consideration) the differences are not really serious. Many are nothing more than minor variations in spelling, grammar, and language, which probably sprang up during the early period of oral transmission and translation. They certainly do not damage gospel credibility. Furthermore, free paraphrasing was normal in the ancient Middle East, where quotation marks did not exist. Even today, people with great powers of recall can seldom produce an exact account of last year's political discussion, last month's motivational lecture, or last week's social conversation. Yet most of us will accept an observer's summary as an accurate account of the important things that were said at each of those events. We intuitively understand that his or her memory cannot give us the accuracy of a transcript. For the same reason, we cannot expect stenographic accuracy from the gospel writers and their eyewitness sources.

When all the trivial variations have been eliminated, what remains is a fairly small number of significant factual differences among the Gospels. Even though they are far outweighed by the number of factual similarities, they do need to be explained.

Perhaps the best way to start is by an analogy. Suppose that four people participate in a transcontinental automobile trip and that each one writes an account of the journey. Each account will describe events that are also in the other three, often in similar— but not identical—language, and occasionally with contradictions about the details. Each account will also describe events that were *not* recorded by any other participant. When the four accounts are bound together they will provide an accurate history of the trip, each reflecting the viewpoints and interests of the particular author. The accuracy will not be diminished by differences in the authors' selections and descriptions of events. In fact, if the accounts were virtually identical, we would assume that they were really just a single account written by a committee of four, each member having altered some of his own perceptions and recollections in the interest of harmony. This would reduce our confidence in the independence, the accuracy, and the richness of the complete journal. It would even make us wonder why the four participants didn't just openly produce a single, blended account of their journey.

So it is with the gospel accounts. They are not verbatim copies of each other. They do contain factual differences. But this does not mean that they are unreliable records of historical events. The very fact that they are *not* some slickly produced work by an official committee allows us to be confident of their accuracy. Word-for-word duplication would stimulate suspicion, eroding the evidentiary strength of four independent Gospels and giving all of us reason to doubt their historical accuracy.

But that's not the way it worked. Even if Mark's gospel was written first, and was then used by Matthew, Luke, and John, all four gospel writers certainly drew upon eyewitness reports. They may also have drawn upon written collections of Jesus' sayings, and perhaps upon contemporaneous written notes of his teachings. This is not to say that all four authors had full access to a common body of source material. They probably did not, especially since they seem to have written in different locales and at different times. But each author must have had access to at least some of the sources. So, having selected material from his common and separate sources, he wrote according to his best understanding of the facts and his editorial objectives for the anticipated audience.

Christians maintain that the Gospels (as well as the rest of the Bible) were inspired by God.[35] This does not mean God physically dictated the Gospels the way a person today would dictate to a stenographer. The gospel authors were not ancient versions of modern court reporters. Rather, as a pastor friend of mine once commented, the Bible (including the Gospels) was "divinely inspired and culturally conditioned." It was written by many individuals over many centuries and in many locales. Even within the short time frame of Jesus' life, the Gospels have room for factual differences, for uncertainties, and for interpretations. Reasonable people can differ about these details. But differences and uncertainties do not dilute the Gospels' overriding accuracy and reliability. In fact, assuming that God inspired the original authors to seek out the best documentary and eyewitness recollections, he may have actually *wanted* them to differ in the details and in the selections of events to write about. He could have done this in order to establish credibility in the eyes of people just like me. If I were faced with a tidy package of four neat and synchronized Gospels, I would surely succumb to the nagging suspicion that they had been homogenized by some ancient advertising executive in first-century Jerusalem. Such a production would not ring nearly as true as the individual Gospels that have come down to us.

So what types of factual differences are found among the three synoptic Gospels?

One type involves differences in the chronological order of events. At first glance, this may seem to present a problem. However, the notion of strict chronological order probably never even entered the minds of the gospel authors. Their accounts were assembled for the purpose of describing the pertinent events of

---

[35] 2 Timothy 3:16.

Jesus' ministry and the content of his teachings. Their sequences were often arranged by topic, not by chronology. The Gospels simply do not purport to be strict, day-to-day diaries of what Jesus did and what he said. In that sense, they are more akin to anthologies than to biographies.

Another type of difference involves the omission by one synoptic gospel author of an event that is included by one or both of the others. An example is Matthew's story about events following Jesus' birth: the Star of Bethlehem, the Wise Men from the East, Joseph and Mary's flight with Jesus into Egypt, and Herod's slaughter of young boys in Bethlehem.[36] None of this material appears in Mark or Luke. So does it constitute a factual contradiction? No. Mark and Luke may not have known the story. Or they may have considered it unimportant. Or their omission may have been for some other reason, like the need to develop a particular theme. Nobody really knows. But we do know that omissions like this do not constitute factual contradictions. Going back to the illustration of an automobile trip across the country, we would not label the trip journal as fictional just because one—and only one—participant mentioned a meteor shower in Colorado, or a roadside encounter with an Irish family in Kansas, or an unexpected detour to avoid a thunderstorm in Missouri. Similarly, the gospels of Mark and Luke can hardly be mistrusted for simply omitting a story that Matthew decided to include.

A third type of difference stems from the fact that normal literary practice in ancient times was to paraphrase or abridge. In all likelihood many of Jesus' teachings, as recorded in the Gospels, were paraphrased and condensed from the longer sermons that he delivered orally. On other occasions, parts of several sermons that Jesus had spoken orally at different times and in different places were probably compiled into a single written sermon. The Sermon on the Mount is an example. It is usually quoted from Matthew's version, even though Luke reports a similar, shorter version, sometimes called the Sermon on the Plain.[37] The reason for the

---

[36] Matthew 2:1–18.
[37] Matthew 5:1–7:29; Luke 6:17–49; 12:22–31, 33–34.

difference must lie in the fact that Jesus delivered many messages during his two or three years of traveling throughout Galilee. Most likely, Matthew and Luke extracted the essence of some of these messages (each using his own selections) and, to give coherence, condensed them into a single sermon. Should this cause a problem? Not really. Jesus' teaching was extensive, and the gospel techniques of paraphrasing, condensing, and compiling were neither uncommon nor unreliable.

Turning now from these various categories of differences among the synoptic Gospels, we should look briefly at John's gospel. It differs in style and chronology from the other three. Most of the differences can be explained by the likelihood that John wrote his gospel (or supervised its writing) after he had become an old man living on the west coast of modern Turkey. He painted his picture of Jesus from the vantage point of a long life, which had given him time to consider and prioritize the facts and their implications. He may also have had independent sources that were unavailable to the synoptic authors.

With regard to the specific factual differences between John and the synoptics, most of them relate to events that are omitted from John and included in the synoptics, or vice versa. These differences can typically be explained by the fact that John focused on Jesus' ministry in Judea, while the snyoptics focused on his ministry in Galilee. This does not create any problem of credibility. To the extent that differences in chronology do exist between John and the synoptics, most have been reconciled by scholars, although admittedly a few uncertainties remain.[38] Finally, it is important to note that John, who wrote the most theological of the four Gospels, includes more geographical details than does Matthew, Mark, or Luke. Many of these details have been independently corroborated (as will be reviewed in chapter five), thus dem-

---

[38] For example, the synoptics state that Jesus drove the moneychangers out of the temple during the final week of his life (Matthew 21:12–13; Mark 11:15–17; Luke 19:45–46). But John places the event at the start of Jesus' ministry (John 2:13–16). Various harmonizations have been proposed, but none has gained universal acceptance.

onstrating that John was familiar with Judean geography and accurately incorporated it into his gospel.

To summarize: Few of the factual differences among the four Gospels seem to constitute flat contradictions. And those that do exist are not a serious impediment to gospel credibility. In fact, we are indeed fortunate to have such a reasonable balance between diversity and uniformity among the four gospel accounts. They supplement each other as four individual and honest perceptions of what really happened in Galilee and Judea nearly two thousand years ago.

INTERNAL EVIDENCE OF GOSPEL CREDIBILITY

Several items of internal evidence endow the gospel pages with an aura of credibility. Most of it consists of incidents that embarrassingly depict Jesus' disciples as flawed men. Their human frailties and weaknesses are vividly described. Such incidents would hardly have been included if the Gospels were mere fictional stories. So their very presence constitutes a distinct category of evidence supporting the historical reliability of the gospel accounts. A few illustrations should suffice.

First, we are told that the disciples were a bit on the dense side and that Jesus became miffed at them for failing to understand his teachings. For example, after telling them the parable of the sower and then realizing that they just didn't get the point, Jesus became exasperated and asked:

Don't you understand this parable? How then will you understand *any* parable?[39]

Second, the Gospels allow us to witness unseemly displays of pride and ego when the disciples jockeyed for favorable positions among Jesus' followers. One example occurred at the Last Supper, when:

---

[39] Mark 4:13 (emphasis added).

> a dispute arose among them as to which of them was considered to be the greatest.[40]

Similarly, two of the most prominent disciples once asked Jesus:

> to do for us whatever we ask. . .Let one of us sit at your right and the other at your left in your glory.[41]

Not even the mother of these two disciples was immune from a display of pride. She asked Jesus to:

> grant that one of these two sons of mine may sit at your right and the other at your left in your kingdom.[42]

The other ten disciples were "indignant with the two brothers" when they heard about it.

Third, our attention is riveted by the famous gospel story about the sudden shriveling of Peter's loyalty. After Jesus was arrested in Gethsemane, Peter three times denied that he even knew his Lord and friend.[43] Mark's account of the story is particularly significant. As Peter's interpreter, he would have had especially strong motivation to cast Peter in a good light. But he did just the opposite by describing Peter's unbecoming conduct after the arrest.

Fourth, the Gospels tell us that all the disciples behaved with cowardice after Jesus was arrested. Matthew, one of the disciples himself, candidly admits, "all the disciples deserted him and fled."[44] Mark uses nearly identical language.[45]

It is hard to imagine that authors who were contriving a fictional account about Jesus and his followers, or even a sanitized portrayal of them, would have infused the disciples with so many

---

[40] Luke 22:24.

[41] Mark 10:35–37.

[42] Matthew 20:20–24.

[43] Matthew 26:31–35, 69–75; Mark 14:27–31; 66–72; John 18:15–27.

[44] Matthew 26:56.

[45] Mark 14:50.

unpleasant characteristics: dense intellects, large egos, flimsy loyalties, and cowardly behavior. Instead, the authors would have tried to show that the disciples were men who profoundly understood Jesus' teachings, who followed his model of servant ministry, whose dedication to him was unshakable, and who acted bravely in a crisis. But that is not the way the disciples were described. So, by highlighting serious character flaws in these hallowed men, the Gospels ring true.

One other piece of internal evidence deserves mention. All four Gospels describe in detail the role played by Joseph of Arimathea. They identify him as a wealthy member of the Jewish Sanhedrin—Israel's ruling council—who provided the tomb for Jesus and assisted in his burial process. Skeptics tend to ignore this man when they sometimes argue that Jesus' dead body was probably thrown into a common grave for crucified criminals. Authors who were concocting a myth about a private burial would not have assigned such an important role to so prominent a man. If Joseph of Arimathea was a real person—the notable Jew and secret Christian sympathizer described in the Gospels—he would surely have challenged any untrue claims about his complicity in Jesus' burial. And if he was a fictional person, the gospel authors would surely not have been so foolish as to base their entire claim of private burial on a fictitious character whose claimed prominence would guarantee instant exposure of the entire story as a fraud. So Joseph's inclusion in all four Gospels enhances the credibility of the story.

INCORPORATION OF THE FOUR GOSPELS INTO THE NEW TESTAMENT

Sometime around A.D. 100 the four Gospels, along with Paul's letters, were being assembled into a single collection. The exact process and timing of the compilation cannot be precisely reconstructed. But scholars have been able to estimate the events with a reasonable degree of probability.

As noted earlier in this chapter, Matthew's gospel was probably written in Syria or Palestine; Mark's in Rome; Luke's in Rome, Greece, or Turkey; and John's at Ephesus in western Turkey. The

Christian movement had already begun to spread around and out from the eastern Mediterranean coastal area. Copies of the four gospels may have been first compiled into a single collection in order that Christians would not be limited to the particular one that was being used in their own locale.

Citations in the letters of early church leaders like Clement, Ignatius, and Polycarp reveal that by around A.D. 115 the Gospels and Paul's letters were being circulated as a single collection. About thirty years later a man from Asia Minor named Marcion produced a collection consisting of an edited version of Luke's gospel and ten of Paul's letters. Around the same time a Gnostic document entitled *The Gospel of Truth* was written. Discovered in 1945 at the town of Nag Hammadi, about sixty miles up the Nile River from Luxor, it refers to the gospels of Matthew, Luke, and John, to most of Paul's letters, and to the books of Hebrews and Revelation. About A.D. 170, a Syrian Christian named Tatian produced a blended version of the four gospels.[46] Then, sometime around A.D. 200, an unknown compiler prepared a Latin list (which has come down to us as a damaged copy) identifying and commenting on most of the books that are contained in our modern New Testament.[47] Thereafter, during the third century and the early part of the fourth, various church leaders wrote comments about some of the books.

These examples of early references to the New Testament collection do not appear to reflect any official stamp of approval. Instead, the process of collecting the books seems to have been driven by the separate needs of many local Christian churches and individual missionaries. They all wanted to have a reliable record of Jesus' ministry. They also wanted to have the writings of the apostle Paul, Christianity's preeminent missionary and theologian, as well as a few other letters that they considered to be important. No decree was issued setting apart any particular documents to meet these needs. Rather, the four gospel accounts (along with the other

---

[46] It was called the "Diatessaron," meaning "harmony of four."

[47] Named the *Muratorian Fragment*, after the scholar who published it in 1740 from a seventh- or eighth-century codex.

New Testament writings) came to be accepted because scores of individual Christians and local churches, at the grassroots level, considered them to be authentic and authoritative. The critical consideration was apostolic authority. People became satisfied that each of the four gospels had been written by one of the apostles, or by someone who was a close companion of an apostle. Essentially, that's all there was to it.

The first complete list of our modern New Testament books appears to have been prepared in A.D. 367 by Athanasius, Bishop of Alexandria. He specifically identified them as "the books of the New Testament." Other lists were produced during the years that followed. Finally, in A.D. 393 at the Council of Hippo, the organized church officially declared that nothing should be read in churches except the canonical writings, which were identified by name as the twenty-seven books of our modern New Testament. Four years later this decision was confirmed by the Third Council of Carthage. From these two formal church actions, the New Testament officially emerged. But the important point to keep in mind is this: The Councils of Hippo and Carthage did not create anything new. They did not issue imperial edicts out of thin air. Rather, they simply put their stamp of approval on the specific writings that, for many decades, had already been considered authoritative by local churches throughout Christendom.

Chapter Five

✝

EXTERNAL EVIDENCE CORROBORATING THE GOSPEL ACCOUNTS

INTRODUCTION

The gospel pages are not a murky swamp of shadowy stories. On the contrary, they abound with crisp details about the historical settings in which Jesus lived and died. Individual people are named. Geographical places are identified. Man-made structures are mentioned. Specific events are described.

If the gospel authors had been writing exaggeration or fiction, trying to pass it off as historical truth, they would certainly not have sprinkled their accounts with details that could be disputed by the remaining eyewitnesses or by future visitors to the region. Such pilgrims did indeed appear by around A.D. 160, when Melito, Bishop of Sardis (inland from the west coast of modern Turkey) visited Palestine.[1] If the eyewitnesses or pilgrims had observed any major misstatements in the Gospels, the credibility of the authors would have been shattered right from the outset, and the Christian movement would never have gotten underway. So the very fact that the authors incorporated a multitude of historical and geographical details gives strong reason to think that they were trying to write accurate historical accounts and to present honest summaries of Jesus' teachings.

In determining whether they succeeded, we will need to review the independent, external evidence pertaining to factual

---

[1] Jack Finegan, *The Archeology of the New Testament*, rev. ed. (Princeton, NJ: Princeton University Press, 1992), pp. xiv–xv.

statements in the Gospels. If many of the statements are corroborated, and if none are refuted, then we can confidently apply the
face value presumption of historical accuracy to those statements
for which no external evidence has yet been discovered. The greater
the number of corroborated statements, and the fewer the number
of refuted statements, the higher will be our level of confidence in
the statements for which we have no evidence one way or the other.

Before starting, mention should be made of one factor bearing
on the identification of ancient sites. The year A.D. 324 is a sort of
dividing line. Twelve years earlier, in A.D. 312, Constantine, one of
the Roman Empire's several co-rulers, had converted to Christianity. The following year he and one of his co-rulers issued a decree
of religious toleration—the first step toward official recognition of
Christianity. Then, in A.D. 324, he became the sole emperor of the
empire. He immediately began to rebuild the old city of Byzantium
(modern Istanbul) and make it his capital. This brought him geographically closer to the historical roots of Christianity, and it also
eliminated the political primacy of Rome. The Byzantine Empire
had begun.

As soon as Constantine had became sole emperor, the Christians were freed from nearly three centuries of public hostility and
occasional Roman persecution. Some Christians, including
Constantine's elderly mother, Helena, made pilgrimages to Palestine. They searched for Christian historical sites and then memori-
alized them with churches and monuments. However, the zeal of
these Byzantine pilgrims, along with the centuries by which they
were separated from the events of Jesus' life, created the risk that
they would make hasty identifications from slender evidence. So
when the authenticity of Christian sites is being examined, identifications initially made *before* A.D. 324 are probably entitled to a bit
more confidence than those initially made thereafter.

EVIDENCE FOR THE GOSPEL ACCOUNTS OF JESUS' BIRTH AND INFANCY

Matthew and Luke describe events surrounding Jesus' birth
and infancy. One such event, well known to most people, is the

claim that Jesus was born to a virgin—a young woman named Mary—and that conception occurred through God's Holy Spirit.[2] No independent evidence exists to either corroborate or refute this claim. So it really cannot be addressed in this chapter on external evidence. However, the virgin birth does appear in a later discussion about why the gospel miracle stories do not need to impede a step of Christian faith.[3]

Turning then to the rest of what Matthew and Luke wrote, the basic story emerges: A Roman census required Joseph and Mary to leave their home in Nazareth and journey to Joseph's ancestral town of Bethlehem. While they were there, Mary gave birth to Jesus. Sometime later, wise men from the east, responding to a star they had seen in the eastern sky, visited the child in Bethlehem. After they left, Joseph became fearful that King Herod would try to kill Jesus. So the family fled to Egypt. When Herod died, they went home to Nazareth, where Jesus grew to manhood.

A good deal of independent evidence corroborates this story.

Nazareth. According to Luke's gospel, the story of Jesus begins in Nazareth, where Mary and Joseph lived. Surprisingly, this town is not even mentioned in the Old Testament. Nor is it mentioned by Josephus, whose military headquarters was only three miles away and who listed forty-five other towns in the Galilee area. Even the Jewish Talmud, which names sixty-three Galilean towns, is silent about ancient Nazareth. So its very existence was formerly open to question. But, in 1962, archaeologists excavating at Caesarea (on the Mediterranean coast of Israel) found a fragment of dark gray marble that was dated to about A.D. 300. It contained a Hebrew inscription listing twenty-four priestly families in Galilee and identifying their communities. One of them was Nazareth.

The site of modern Nazareth, which sits on a ridge, just as Luke described,[4] has been archaeologically explored since 1892. In recent years excavations have shown that the area used to be an

---

[2] Matthew 1:18–25; Luke 1:26–38.
[3] See pp. 193–195.
[4] Luke 4:29.

agricultural village, with pottery fragments dating all the way back to 900 B.C. So it was indeed a very old town. And in the first century A.D. it was also a very tiny town, home to perhaps as few as twenty families. Many tombs have been uncovered, four of which had been sealed with rolling stones.[5] Such stones, shaped like large, round disks, were typical of first-century Jewish practice and reminiscent of the type of stone that was probably used to seal up Jesus' own tomb during the same period.

The dominant architectural feature of modern Nazareth is the enormous Basilica of the Annunciation, the fifth consecutive church built on the same site. It commemorates the story about Mary's visit from the angel Gabriel, who announced that she would give birth to a son.[6] Excavations under the modern church have revealed that an early church was built on the site around A.D. 250. It included the grottoes that later generations identified with Joseph and Mary. Many remains of this early church were covered with Byzantine plaster, on which graffiti had been cut. One column bears the partial Greek inscription, ". . .under the holy place of M. . ." Another one shows a similar inscription, ". . .ave [hail] Mary." Both of these inscriptions can be examined today by visitors to Nazareth. The church and the graffiti confirm that, from pre-Byzantine times, this place was being revered as Mary's home.

The census of Quirinius. Luke's gospel reports that, in order to "register" for an empire-wide Roman census, ordered by Caesar Augustus, Joseph and a very pregnant Mary were required to journey to Joseph's hometown of Bethlehem. According to Luke, "this was the first census that took place while Quirinius was governor of Syria."[7] Based on the writings of Josephus, scholars have long known that Quirinius, as the Roman governor of Syria, had conducted a taxation assessment in the Jewish province of Judea in

---

[5] Jack Finegan, *The Archeology of the New Testament*, p. 46.

[6] Luke 1:26–27.

[7] Luke 2:2. Some scholars translate this verse to mean that the census took place "before"—not "while"—Quirinius was governor of Syria. If they are correct, then the whole debate about the year of the census becomes irrelevant.

A.D. 6. But all scholars agree that Jesus was born at least eight years *before* that time. Thus many of them have disputed the accuracy of Luke's reference to Quirinius and the census, thereby casting doubt on Luke's credibility as a reliable historian.

Even if these scholars were right, the reliability of Luke's gospel would not be seriously diminished just because of an erroneous date for the governorship of one peripheral figure on the New Testament stage. However, for two separate reasons, Luke was probably not guilty of an error.[8]

First, archaeologists have uncovered in Antioch two fragments of a Roman inscription. It appears to show that Quirinius did indeed hold some sort of leadership position in Syria around the period from 8 B.C. to 2 B.C.—several years before his official governorship in A.D. 6 and well within the time frame for Jesus' birth. Tacitus reports that this earlier position involved a military mission that Quirinius conducted for the emperor Augustus. It could well have been the "governorship" to which Luke referred. In fact, Luke's Greek word that is translated into English as *governor* can also connote a less official leadership position.

Second, Luke's gospel specifically states that Jesus was born at the time of "the *first* census" during Quirinius's governorship (emphasis added). By contrast, in his book of Acts, Luke uses slightly—but significantly—different language with regard to the well-known census of A.D. 6, quoting Gamaliel's reference to it as "the days of *the* census."[9] If, in his gospel, Luke intended to tie Jesus' birth to the census of A.D. 6, he would simply have adopted the same language he used in Acts and referred to it as "the" census, not the "first" one. But he didn't. So Luke was clearly aware of *two* censuses.

Thus it is fair to draw the following conclusion: As a careful historian, Luke knew that Quirinius was the leader of Syria on two

---

[8] See the discussions in F. F. Bruce, *The New Testament Documents*, pp. 86–87 and Ernest L. Martin, *The Star that Astonished the World*, 2d ed. (Portland, OR: ASK Publications, 1996), pp. 181–199.

[9] Acts 5:37 (emphasis added).

separate occasions, that the well-known census of A.D. 6 occurred during his second (official) governorship, and that the *first* census, at the time of Jesus' birth, occurred during his earlier (unofficial) governorship.

This conclusion is consistent with two other known historical facts. First, late in his reign King Herod was demoted by the emperor Augustus, who informed him that even though the emperor had formerly "used him as his *friend*, he should now use him as his *subject*."[10] This explains why Augustus would have ordered the first census, at the time of Jesus' birth, to be conducted by Quirinius (the Roman leader of Syria), rather than by Herod (who would normally have conducted it as the local king of Judea). Herod needed to get back into Augustus's good graces. So when the first census was ordered in Judea (probably in connection with the 3 B.C. oath of allegiance to Augustus preceding his twenty-fifth anniversary as emperor[11] and the new title, "Father of the Country," bestowed on him by "the entire Roman people"[12]) Herod would not have objected if the Romans wanted to conduct it themselves.

Second, some scholars have questioned the historical accuracy of Luke's comment about a Roman requirement for Mary and Joseph to travel from Nazareth to Bethlehem in order to register for the census. But the fruitful sands of Egypt have produced confirmation of Luke's account in the form of a Roman public notice, dated A.D. 104. It directs all people residing away from their own districts to return immediately in order to register for an enrollment. This is the very sort of requirement that Luke describes as having earlier been imposed on Joseph and Mary, forcing them to undertake a trek to Bethlehem.

On net balance, Luke's account of Quirinius's census is well able to withstand the assaults of its critics.

---

[10] Josephus, "The Antiquities of the Jews" 16.290, *The Works*, p. 443 (emphasis added).

[11] Josephus, "The Antiquities of the Jews" 17.42, *The Works*, p. 453.

[12] Augustus, *Res Gestae*, VI.35, quoted by Ernest L. Martin in *The Star that Astonished the World*, p. 189.

Bethlehem. In his gospel, Luke tells us that Joseph:

> went up from the town of Nazareth in Galilee to Judea, to Beth-
> lehem the town of David, because he belonged to the house and
> line of David. He went there to register with Mary. . .[13]

Bethlehem lies about eighty-five miles south of Nazareth. According to the Old Testament, it was King David's hometown.[14]
We have no direct archaeological evidence that Jesus was born there.
But we do know that the early church leader Justin Martyr, in a
letter to the Roman emperor around A.D. 150, identified Bethlehem as the:

> village in the land of the Jews, thirty-five stadia [about four miles]
> from Jerusalem, in which Jesus Christ was born, as you can learn
> from the census which was taken under Quirinius.[15]

Justin elsewhere refers to the birthplace as a "cave."

Reference to a Bethlehem "cave" also appears in the writings of
Origen, a Christian scholar and philosopher who was born in Egypt
toward the end of the second century A.D. He traveled often to
Palestine. Around A.D. 248, undoubtedly after a personal visit, he
wrote as follows:

> In accordance with the narrative in the gospel regarding [Jesus']
> birth, there is pointed out at Bethlehem the cave where he was
> born, and the manger in the cave where he was wrapped in swad-
> dling clothes. And this site is greatly talked of in surrounding
> places, even among the enemies of the faith.[16]

---

[13] Luke 2:4–5.
[14] 1 Samuel 16:1; 17:58.
[15] "First Apology" 34, Cyril C. Richardson, *Early Christian Fathers*, p. 264.
[16] *Against Celsus*, quoted by Jack Finegan, *The Archeology of the New Testament*, rev. ed., p. 30. Copyright © 1992 by Princeton University Press. Reprinted by permission of Princeton University Press.

These early references to a "cave" seem to conflict with the probability that Jesus was born in a private Bethlehem home.[17] However, the private home could indeed have been a cave. As Professor Jack Finegan points out, "Caves have actually provided habitation and shelter for *persons* and *beasts* in Palestine from ancient times until now."[18]

Less than a hundred years after the time of Origen, the emperor Constantine built the first Church of the Nativity over this cave. When the building was destroyed during the Samaritan revolt in A.D. 529, the emperor Justinian immediately rebuilt it. His church stands to this day. There is no good reason to doubt that it is located over (or at least near) the actual place where Jesus was born.

The year of Jesus' birth. In and of itself, the year of Jesus' birth is not especially important. However, for purposes of looking (in the next subsection) at the evidence for Matthew's Star of Bethlehem story, it becomes vital. The year has now been determined by a new and persuasive historical/astronomical analysis. It will only be summarized here, because the details would be too lengthy to explore.

Twelve early authors, writing between A.D. 170 and A.D. 585, mentioned the year of Jesus' birth.[19] One of them placed it in 4 B.C., one in 4/3 B.C., and one in A.D. 1. The other nine placed it between 3 and 1 B.C. Yet today most scholars disregard these ancient writers, claiming that Jesus must have been born several years earlier—in 6 or 5 B.C. They reach this conclusion because King Herod is assumed to have died in 4 B.C., and Matthew's gospel explicitly states that Jesus was born while Herod was still alive.[20]

---

[17] See pp. 45–46.

[18] *The Archeology of the New Testament*, p. 30 (emphasis added). Reprinted by permission of Princeton University Press.

[19] Jack Finegan, *Handbook of Biblical Chronology* (Princeton, NJ: Princeton University Press, 1964), pp. 222–230.

[20] Matthew 2:1.

Why is Herod's death supposed to have occurred in 4 B.C.? Primarily because of Josephus's report that he died shortly after an eclipse of the moon, which scholars have long identified as the partial lunar eclipse on March 13 in 4 B.C. However, a recent re-evaluation of the historical evidence has disputed this traditional identification of the eclipse and has concluded that Herod did not die until early in 1 B.C.[21] If this is true, then the ancient writers were quite correct in placing Jesus' birth sometime in 3/2 B.C.

Why did scholars originally select the partial lunar eclipse on March 13 in 4 B.C. as the one to which Josephus referred? Primarily because Herod's three sons, who divided up the kingdom upon his death, seem to have started their own reigns in 4 B.C. However, this does not dispose of the issue. According to the earliest manuscripts of Josephus, one of the sons, Philip, appears to have actually started his reign in about 1 B.C.[22] And, as was common in the Middle East, the other two sons, Antipas and Archelaus, could have retroactively dated the start of their own reigns three years before their father's death. This would have been at the time when Herod was politically demoted by Caesar Augustus from "friend" to "subject" and when he elevated another of his sons, Antipater (whom he later executed), to the status of co-ruler.[23] Antipas and Archelaus would surely have been ashamed of their father's demotion by Augustus, and would probably have been angry over their father's elevation of Antipater, whom they had reason to despise. So they

---

[21] Ernest L. Martin, *The Star that Astonished the World*; see also John Mosley, *The Christmas Star* (Los Angeles: Griffith Observatory, 1987). This re-dating of Herod's death by three years is not the only recent instance of a proposed change in traditional historical chronologies. Egyptologist and historian David Rohl argues that traditional dates for the Israelite bondage and Egyptian dynasties, including such figures as Joseph, Moses, and the Pharaoh of the Exodus, should be adjusted by several hundred years. David M. Rohl, *Pharaohs and Kings* (New York: Crown Publishers, 1995).

[22] Ernest L. Martin, *The Star that Astonished the World*, pp. 112–113; Josephus, "The Antiquities of the Jews" 18.106, *The Works*, p. 483.

[23] Josephus, "The Antiquities of the Jews" 16.290, 17.3, *The Works*, pp. 443, 451.

would have been motivated to retroactively incorporate the co-ruler period into their own reigns, meaning that Herod himself could have died anytime during the first few years of those reigns.

Once this possibility was recognized, astronomers who were searching for the lunar eclipse connected with Herod's death were no longer limited to a period prior to the end of 4 B.C.[24] They could search for eclipses up to three years later. By doing so, they learned that no lunar eclipses took place in 3 B.C. or 2 B.C., but that a full eclipse did occur on January 9/10 in 1 B.C. A comparison of these two eclipses—the traditional one in 4 B.C. and the newly identified one in 1 B.C.—furnishes two strong reasons for deciding that the 1 B.C. eclipse is actually the one that Josephus associated with Herod's death.

The first reason is simple and straightforward. In all of his voluminous writings, Josephus mentioned only one lunar eclipse. It was more likely to have been the spectacular *total* eclipse of 1 B.C. than the inconspicuous *partial* one of 4 B.C.

The second reason is more complicated, but also more powerful. Josephus describes a series of complex events that occurred between the lunar eclipse and the feast of Passover: King Herod, being gravely ill, made a fifty-mile round-trip journey from Jericho to therapeutic mineral baths near the Dead Sea. He assembled the principal Jewish elders from throughout the nation and imprisoned them in Jericho's hippodrome. He had one of his sons executed. Five days later Herod died. The soldiers then promised allegiance to his son Archelaus, the new king of Judea and Samaria. Archelaus made "sumptuous" funeral arrangements. The funeral procession, including the whole army, slowly traversed the twenty miles to Herod's burial place near Bethlehem. Archelaus then remained in mourning for seven days, after which he transacted

---

[24] Astronomers (and even the rest of us, if we purchase sky map programs for our home computers) can reconstruct the sky for any date and time in the past and from any vantage point on Earth. Planetarium shows are built around this capability.

numerous specified items of government business, including actions on various petitions from the populace.[25]

The key to the dating of Herod's death lies in Josephus's statement that *all* these time-consuming events occurred *prior* to the Passover that followed the lunar eclipse. In 4 B.C. this period of time was only twenty-nine days—not nearly long enough for everything to have transpired. By contrast, in 1 B.C. the Passover followed the lunar eclipse by a full three months—ample time for all the activities to be completed.

So the redating of King Herod's death from 4 B.C. to 1 B.C. is probably correct. It comports with the relative prominence of the two lunar eclipses, and it provides adequate time for all the events described by Josephus to have occurred after the eclipse and before the Passover. It also clears up a long-standing mystery of Roman history. Josephus reports that shortly after Herod's death a Jewish revolt escalated into a major Palestinian conflict.[26] Several Roman legions from Syria, under the command of Quintilius Varus, were sent to crush it. If Herod had died early in 4 B.C., this conflict would have occurred during that same year. But, curiously, there is no Roman record of such a war anytime between 4 B.C. and 1 B.C. Instead, during that period, the Roman army was being downsized, and the emperor Augustus was receiving no imperial acclamations, something he would normally have been given after a victory abroad. These strange silences are best explained if Herod's death and the ensuing revolt actually took place in 1 B.C.—the same year in which known military conflicts were erupting in the Middle East, the downsizing of the army had ceased, and Augustus was about to receive his fifteenth imperial acclamation.

With Herod's death occurring early in 1 B.C., the date of Jesus' birth can now be reasonably estimated as a year or two earlier, i.e., in 3/2 B.C. Astronomers have thus been able to search for the famous Star of Bethlehem within a new three-year window, one that

---

[25] "The Antiquities of the Jews" 17.167–213, *The Works*, pp. 462–465.
[26] "The Antiquities of the Jews" 17.250–298, *The Works*, pp. 468–471.

was ignored during the centuries when Herod was assumed to have died in 4 B.C. and Jesus was assumed to have been born in 6/5 B.C.

This brings us to the real purpose for emphasizing the date of Jesus' birth.

The Star and the Wise Men. Matthew's familiar story about the Star of Bethlehem and the visit of the Wise Men[27] has often been considered legendary. Certainly it does not appear to have any particular theological importance. Consisting of twelve little verses, it simply sets the stage for the flight of Joseph, Mary, and Jesus into Egypt, where they remained until after Herod died.[28] But if these events really happened—if there really was a star and a group of Wise Men—then Matthew's gospel gains some credibility. This means that his story needs to be investigated.

Who were the Wise Men, or "Magi," as Matthew calls them?[29] Source documents are meager, but the early Greek historian Herodotus identifies them as a respected tribe of priests in ancient Persia. They practiced what today we call astrology, and from their name comes our English word *magic*. Because of the Israelite exile to Babylon in the sixth century B.C., the Magi had undoubtedly become familiar with Jewish beliefs and prophecies, including Daniel's prophecy of a messiah,[30] which also seems to have been known to the Romans.[31] This familiarity would have been part of the Magi's motive for responding to a "star" they had seen rising in the east.

---

[27] Matthew 2:1–12.

[28] Egypt was not an unusual place for them to go, since Alexandria had long been home to a large number of Jews.

[29] Matthew does not specify how many Wise Men traveled to Jerusalem and Bethlehem. The traditional number of three is simply an assumption that each man brought one of the three types of gifts to which Matthew refers, i.e., gold, incense, and myrrh.

[30] Daniel 9:25.

[31] Tacitus, *Histories* 5.13, Great Books of the Western World, vol. 15, trans. Alfred John Church and William Jackson Brodribb (Chicago, IL: Encyclopaedia Britannica, 1952), p. 298; Suetonius, "Vespasian" 4, *The Twelve Caesars*, p. 281.

What was that "star"? For a long time most scholars and astronomers, working with an assumed birth date for Jesus around 6/5 B.C., had sensibly dismissed comets and exploding stars as candidates. Instead, they had focused their attention on three conjunctions of the planets Jupiter and Saturn, which occurred over a six-month span in 7 B.C. However, as a candidate for the Star of Bethlehem, this triple conjunction has always seemed suspect. The two planets were never closer together than 1° (two diameters of the full moon), and neither of them had any astrological connection with the Jewish nation. So the Magi would not likely have described this pair of planets as a single "star"—much less one that possessed significance for the Jews. Nevertheless, until recently no other candidates existed.

Now, however, astronomers are no longer limited to a search of the sky before 6/5 B.C. They can examine the three-year period preceding Herod's newly redated death—the period from 4 B.C. to 1 B.C. Having done so, they can confidently identify the Star of Bethlehem: It was the planet Jupiter.

Here is how many planetariums are now showing Matthew's story.[32] On the early morning of August 12 in 3 B.C., Magi in the region of Babylon would have seen in the east an unusual and startlingly close conjunction between the planets Jupiter and Venus, the two brightest "stars" in the sky. They were only 0.07° apart, one-seventh the diameter of a full moon. The Magi would surely have taken notice, since Jupiter was astrologically considered the "king" planet, and Venus was the planet of femininity. Moreover, the conjunction took place in the region of the sky where the constellation of Leo the Lion was positioned. Leo was astrologically associated with the Jewish tribe of Judah. So ancient Middle Eastern astrologers, like the Magi, would have concluded that a royal birth might be happening among the Jews.

---

[32] One such planetarium is the Griffith Observatory in Los Angeles. It completely changed its traditional Christmas Star program, which formerly described the triple conjunction of Jupiter and Saturn in 7 B.C.

This conclusion would have been reinforced during the ensuing months, when Jupiter passed through the constellation of Leo three separate times, always coming very close to its brightest star, Regulus. These three consecutive approaches to Regulus resulted from Jupiter's normal, periodic retrograde motion against the background of the stars. This motion, well known to modern astronomers, occurs because Jupiter's orbit is far outside the earth's orbit, and Jupiter is moving slower than the earth is. As a result, when we look at Jupiter over several consecutive nights, it appears to progress further to the *east* each night against the background of the stationary stars. However, the speedier Earth periodically passes the slower Jupiter. When it does so, Jupiter's normal easterly progression is reversed for a viewer on Earth. Against the starry background, Jupiter appears to slow down, stop, and then start moving to the *west*. This "retrograde" motion continues for several months, until the earth has completely passed the giant planet. Then Jupiter once again appears to slow down, stop, and resume its normal *easterly* motion through the stars. This astronomical phenomenon is not easy to explain in words, but it does take place at regular intervals.[33]

So within a span of nine months the Magi had watched their king planet, Jupiter, pass through a spectacular conjunction with Venus, followed by three close approaches to Regulus, the brightest star in the constellation of the Jews. Then, a month later, came a rare and even more extraordinary astronomical event: Early one evening Jupiter and Venus approached each other again, this time in the western sky (toward Jerusalem, as viewed from Babylon). The two came so close together that they appeared to the naked eye as a single planet. It occurred on June 17 in 2 B.C., shortly before 9:00 P.M., Babylonian time. Jupiter and Venus were only 0.01° apart—one-fiftieth the diameter of a full moon. Even with binoculars they would have appeared as a single, brilliant point of light. In fact, a telescope positioned on the earth's equator that evening

---

[33] An excellent explanatory diagram can be found in Ernest L. Martin, *The Star that Astonished the World*, p. 58.

would have shown the two planetary discs as slightly overlapping—
something so rare that it happened most recently in the year 1818
and will not happen again until 2065.

Suffice to say, this second conjunction of Jupiter and Venus
would have removed any lingering doubts for the Magi. Something important—most likely a royal birth—was taking place in
the Jewish nation. So they assembled a caravan and headed for
Jerusalem, some seven or eight hundred miles away by the normal
route. On August 27, about the time they must have gotten underway, the night sky adorned their journey with a celestial confirmation: Four of the planets—Mercury, Venus, Mars, and
Jupiter—clustered into an unusually tight group in the Jewish constellation of Leo.

The Magi would probably have arrived in Jerusalem in the late
autumn of 2 B.C. According to Matthew, they met with King Herod
and learned (or were reminded) about the Jewish prophecy fore-
telling the birth of the Messiah in Bethlehem, just five miles south
of Jerusalem. So they made the short trip. Matthew tells us that:

> the star they had seen in the east went ahead of them until it
> stopped over the place where the child was.[34]

At this point skeptics joyfully scoff at the whole story. Everyone
knows that a star cannot stand still over some particular place on
Earth. However, according to Matthew, is that what the Magi had
really seen? Probably not.

In mid-December of 2 B.C. the planet Jupiter was just starting
its periodic retrograde motion. It was being passed by the earth. As
the Magi looked south from Jerusalem, at their customary early
morning viewing time, they would have seen Jupiter straight ahead,
directly above the town of Bethlehem. The planet would not have
been standing still in a terrestrial sense, since we know that the
entire night sky constantly rotates above the ground from east to
west. But, *against the background of the stars*, Jupiter did indeed

---

[34] Matthew 2:9.

stand perfectly still for several consecutive nights as it was reversing direction from a normal easterly path to a retrograde westerly one. This is what the Magi would have meant by saying it had "stopped." They were speaking as astrologers/astronomers, not as geographers.[35]

So when Matthew wrote his gospel (between A.D. 60 and 85), he correctly reported what his sources had revealed about the Magi's observation some seven decades earlier. He may not have understood exactly what they meant, but he seems to have stated it accurately. His story of the Star of Bethlehem and the Wise Men has a firm historical and astronomical foundation.

EVIDENCE FOR THE GOSPEL ACCOUNTS OF JESUS' LIFE

The gospel stories about Jesus' life and teachings are geographically set in the part of the world we know today as Israel, or Palestine. In Jesus' time it was divided into various regions, such as Judea, Samaria, and Galilee. The Gospels refer to many places that are still well known, such as the Sea of Galilee (a triangular lake, about fourteen miles long), the River Jordan (flowing south from Mount Hermon, through the Sea of Galilee, to the Dead Sea), the city of Jerusalem, and the Temple Mount. The Gospels also refer to a number of well known historical people, such as the various Caesars, who ruled the Roman Empire, and the members of the Herod family, who ruled in Israel/Palestine. By contrast, however, many of the places and people mentioned in the Gospels are not so abundantly verified outside the pages of Christian history.

This section summarizes the external evidence, both manuscript and archaeological, that bears on these sometimes obscure places and people. We begin with a man whose name is well known.

John the Baptist. Luke dates the ministry of John the Baptist, a conspicuous figure in all four gospels, from a time when certain

---

[35] Anyone with a proper astronomical program on his or her home computer can reproduce and print out this exact event, just as it happened back in 2 B.C.

particular rulers were in power: Tiberius Caesar, Pontius Pilate, Herod Antipas (tetrarch of Galilee), and his brother Philip (tetrarch of Iturea and Traconitis).[36] All these men, and the periods of their rule, are known from ancient history. By determining when their reigns overlapped, scholars were able to fix the start of John the Baptist's ministry at A.D. 25/26. This date formerly posed a problem, since Luke identifies one other contemporary ruler: Lysanias, tetrarch of Abilene (a region northwest of Damascus). The only such man known to historians was King Lysanias, who was executed by Marc Antony at the behest of Cleopatra in 36 B.C.—about sixty years too early for John the Baptist. However, archaeology came to the rescue and verified Luke's accuracy. A Greek inscription for a temple dedication was discovered northwest of Damascus, in the area of ancient Abilene. It referred to "Lysanias the Tetrarch" and was dated between A.D. 14 and 29—right in line with the dates in Luke's chronology.[37] So John the Baptist, if he actually existed, probably did begin his ministry in A.D. 25/26.

The external direct evidence for John's historical existence is provided by Josephus. After describing the defeat of Herod Antipas's army at the hands of Aretas, the king of Arabia Petrea, Josephus wrote as follows about John's bloody fate:

> Now, some of the Jews thought that the destruction of Herod's army came. . .as a punishment of what he did against John, that was called the *Baptist*; . . .who was a good man, and commanded the Jews to exercise virtue. . .Herod, who feared lest the great influence John had over the people might put it into his power and inclination to raise a rebellion. . ., thought it best, by putting him to death, to prevent any mischief he might cause. . . Accordingly he was sent a prisoner. . .to Macherus, the castle . . .and was there put to death.[38]

---

[36] Luke 3:1. The title *tetrarch* is a Greek word meaning "ruler."

[37] F. F. Bruce, "Archaeological Confirmation of the New Testament," *Revelation and the Bible*, ed. Carl F. H. Henry (Grand Rapids, MI: Baker Book House, 1958), pp. 326–327.

[38] Josephus, "The Antiquities of the Jews" 18.116–119, *The Works*, p. 484.

This passage corroborates the gospel accounts of John's ministry and death. The only differences are that the Gospels attribute John's death to his criticism of Antipas's marriage to his brother's wife, and they state that the execution itself took place at the insistence of the wife's daughter.[39] But these are simply observations that supplement the agreed-upon facts. It should be noted that Josephus nowhere connects John the Baptist with either Jesus or the Christian movement. So his description of John is independent corroboration for the gospel accounts.

Capernaum. The Gospels identify a town called Capernaum as the place that Jesus used as a headquarters for his ministry in the Galilee area. It was a fishing community, situated on the northwest shore of the lake. Peter had a house there, which he evidently shared with his mother-in-law,[40] providing a place for the band of disciples to sleep and eat. Jesus taught at the town's synagogue, which had been built for the people by a Roman centurion.[41]

Archaeologists first identified and explored the site of Capernaum in 1838. Based on the coins that have been found there, the town existed in the second century B.C. But it was abandoned in the seventh century A.D., never to be rebuilt. In the early 1920s, a white limestone synagogue was uncovered. Dated somewhere between the second and fourth centuries A.D., it could not have been the one where Jesus taught. However, more recent excavations in the 1970s and 1980s have revealed that the limestone structure was built directly atop (and congruent with) an earlier building, which consisted of native black basalt. Based on pottery and coins found in its foundation, this earlier building has been dated to the first century A.D.

The people who constructed the later building clearly venerated the earlier one. They imported expensive limestone for the new construction, and they took care not to disturb the foundation walls of the earlier building. They even carved one of the new

---

[39] Matthew 14:3–12; Mark 1:14, 6:17–29; Luke 3:19–20; John 3:24.

[40] Matthew 8:14–15; Mark 1:29–31; Luke 4:38–39.

[41] Mark 1:21; Luke 7:1–5.

limestone steps into a special shape so it could be fitted like a cap directly over an undisturbed basalt step (depicted on front cover photograph). So the original basalt building must have been Capernaum's synagogue in Jesus' day. The reverence shown by the later builders makes it probable that they were Jewish Christians.

Between the synagogue and the lakeshore, about a hundred yards away, the archaeologists, in 1968, uncovered about a dozen small, connected dwellings from the first century B.C. The mortarless basalt rock walls would not have supported heavy roofing. So mud/straw-covered tree branches probably formed the roofs, thus illuminating the gospel story of a paralytic man being lowered through the roof to be healed by Jesus.[42]

One of these ancient houses received special treatment sometime during the first century A.D., when its original earth/pebble floor was covered by several layers of crushed imported limestone. During the next three hundred years the walls in the largest room of the house received at least three decorative plasterings, as disclosed by hundreds of fragments dated as early as A.D. 175. Many of the plaster fragments include graffiti in Greek, Syriac, Hebrew, and Latin, incised by early pilgrims from various countries. And some of them bear the incised names of Jesus and Peter.

The inference is clear: This particular house and room were revered from the first century A.D. onward as the dwelling of Peter and his houseguest, Jesus. The inference is strengthened by the fact that early in the Byzantine era, around A.D. 350, the house received a new arched ceiling, additional rooms, and a four-sided exterior wall. A sacred complex was thereby created, nearly a hundred feet square and separated from the rest of the houses in the town. It was doubtless the church described in A.D. 381–84 by the early pilgrim Aetheria, who wrote:

---

[42] Mark 2:4.

In Capernaum, moreover, out of the house of the first of the apostles [Peter] a church has been made, the walls of which still stand just as they were. Here the Lord cured the paralytic.[43]

It is fair to state that the various gospel stories of events at Capernaum are corroborated by the archaeological excavations.

Magdala. One of the well-known figures in the Gospels is Mary Magdalene. She was a faithful follower of Jesus, right up to his crucifixion, burial, and resurrection.[44] Her home was undoubtedly in the ancient town of Magdala,[45] which lies on the northwest shore of the Sea of Galilee. Excavations at the site in the 1970s uncovered a Jewish synagogue from the first century A.D.

About a mile north of the site, during a 1986 drought that lowered the water level in the lake, the remains of an old boat were exposed offshore. The vessel was about twenty-seven feet long, eight feet wide, and five feet deep, and it appears to have had a mast and a large stern platform. Carbon-14 testing showed it to be from the time of Jesus. If this was a typical Galilean fishing boat of that time, it would have been large enough to carry Jesus and his twelve disciples around the Sea of Galilee. It would even have given Jesus ample space for sleeping on a cushion in the stern, as described by Mark.[46]

Bethany. The village of Bethany is mentioned twelve times in the Gospels. John places it about two miles from Jerusalem,[47] a

---

[43] Quoted by Jack Finegan, *The Archeology of the New Testament*, p. 110. Reprinted by permission of Princeton University Press. Less than a hundred years later all the private houses in this part of Capernaum were torn down and replaced by an octagonal church with a mosaic pavement. In A.D. 570 this new "basilica" was mentioned in the record of an anonymous pilgrim from Piacenza.

[44] Matthew 27:56, 61; Mark 15:40, 47, 16:1, 9; Luke 24:10; John 19:25, 20:1, 18.

[45] The modern village of Migdal, and referred to by a slightly different name in Matthew 15:39.

[46] Mark 4:38.

[47] John 11:18.

location confirmed by the early church historian Eusebius around A.D. 330, and by the reports of two early pilgrims who wrote shortly thereafter. One was the anonymous Bordeaux Pilgrim (A.D. 333), who identified the town as Bethany and as the place of the crypt where Lazarus had been laid. The other was Aetheria (A.D. 381–384), who identified the place as Lazarium, obviously derived from Lazarus's name. His name is also the source of the town's old Arabic designation: el-'Azariye (place of Lazarus). This change of Bethany's name during the early centuries must have commemorated some exceptional event involving Lazarus. The gospel account of Jesus raising him from the dead would surely qualify.

Today the village of Bethany still exists, two miles east of Jerusalem on the road to Jericho. Archaeological excavations around 1950 revealed that it was continuously inhabited from the sixth century B.C. all the way to the fourteenth century A.D. Among the artifacts uncovered were a coin of Herod the Great and another coin from the time of Pontius Pilate. This is certainly the same community where John claims that Jesus raised Lazarus from the dead[48] and where the Gospels state that Jesus lived during the last week before his crucifixion.[49]

The Lazarus story goes far back in historical records. Writing about Bethany in A.D. 330, Eusebius says, "the place of Lazarus is still pointed out even until now."[50] This is typical language for describing a tradition of very long standing. In fact, Lazarus's tomb is still being shown to tourists today. They enter it by descending twenty-two steps from the modern street level into an underground chamber, from which two additional steps descend through an *opening in the floor* to a five-foot corridor leading to the tomb itself. This unusual layout corresponds precisely with John's gospel,

---

[48] John 11:1–44.
[49] Matthew 21:17, 26:6; Mark 11:11–12, 14:3; John 12:1.
[50] Eusebius, *Onomasticon*, quoted by Jack Finegan, *The Archeology of the New Testament*, p. 157.

which describes the tomb as "a cave with a stone *laid across* the entrance."[51]

The Pool of Bethesda. John's gospel describes how Jesus healed a man who had been an invalid for thirty-eight years. He did so near Jerusalem's Sheep Gate, at:

> a pool, which in Aramaic is called Bethesda and which is surrounded by five covered colonnades. Here a great number of disabled people used to lie.[52]

This would have been an unusual pool, with five—rather than the normal four—covered colonnades. However, in the Copper Scroll (one of the Dead Sea Scrolls), written between A.D. 25 and 68, archaeologists have discovered that the Pool of Bethesda was described as twin pools. It was similarly described by Eusebius in A.D. 330, by the Bordeaux Pilgrim in A.D. 333, and by Cyril, Bishop of Jerusalem, in A.D. 348. So John was obviously describing two pools, not just one. But for a long time nobody knew exactly where they were.

Then in 1957–1962, during archaeological excavations begun many years earlier, two enormous pools were discovered side by side in northeastern Jerusalem. Separated by a dike twenty feet wide (John's fifth colonnade), the adjacent pools were roughly rectangular in shape. The northern one averaged about 169 by 131 feet, while the larger southern one averaged about 202 by 160 feet. These were huge pools indeed, with more than 5,000 square yards of total surface area. Amidst the rubble, archaeologists also came across remnants of the ancient Aesclepium, a Hellenistic sanctuary for the sick, named after the Greek god of medicine.[53] So it

---

[51] John 11:38 (emphasis added). This would *not* have been the type of "rolling" stone that, according to the synoptic Gospels, was later placed in front of Jesus' own tomb. Examples of such rolling stones have been archaeologically uncovered just a short distance from Bethany.

[52] John 5:2–3.

[53] John Romer, *Testament* (New York, NY: Henry Holt and Company, 1988), p. 162.

would have been perfectly normal for Jesus to find at this place an invalid who had been seeking a cure for thirty-eight years among the many other disabled people who, according to John, used to lie there.

Thus John's puzzling description of the five-sided Hellenistic healing pool has been verified archaeologically.

The Pool and tower of Siloam. In John's gospel we read that Jesus healed a blind man by spitting on the ground, putting mud on the man's eyes, and then telling him to go and "wash in the pool of Siloam" (a word which John tells us means *Sent*).[54]

This pool, still in use today, is the place into which Hezekiah's tunnel brings water from the Spring of Gihon, outside the old city walls. The tunnel, 1,750 feet long, was constructed in 701 B.C. as a means of securing the city's water supply during times of siege.[55] In 1880 a Hebrew inscription was found on the wall of the tunnel, about twenty feet before it emerges into the Pool of Siloam, describing how it was dug by two teams of excavators, who worked from opposite ends and met in the middle of the mountain. About 260 years later, in connection with Nehemiah's rebuilding of the city walls, "the wall of the Pool of Siloam" was repaired.[56] The pool was subsequently identified by Josephus (who called it a "fountain"), by the Bordeaux Pilgrim (A.D. 333), and by various other visitors to Jerusalem in the early centuries. Excavations in 1897 showed that the pool was in a square court, about seventy-two feet across and surrounded by an arcade. It is significantly smaller today.

Close by the Pool of Siloam, archaeologists have uncovered the foundation of a round tower. Probably dating from the second century B.C., it is very likely the structure referred to by Jesus, when he described "those eighteen who died when the tower in Siloam fell on them."[57]

---

[54] John 9:6–7.

[55] Described in the Old Testament. 2 Chronicles 32:30.

[56] Described in the Old Testament. Nehemiah 3:15.

[57] Luke 13:4–5.

All in all, strong evidence confirms that John and Luke identified real, historical structures in their accounts of Jesus and the place called "Siloam."

The Gospels tell us that Jesus spent the last week of his life in and around Jerusalem. Along with his disciples, he had journeyed south from Galilee, taken up quarters with Lazarus's family in Bethany, made a triumphal entry into Jerusalem, taught in the Temple area, and overturned the money changers' tables. Then he gathered with the disciples for a final supper, after which they went to an olive grove called Gethsemane. There he was arrested. After several trial-like proceedings during the night and the next morning, including a final one before the Roman governor Pontius Pilate, he was crucified, dying after about six hours on the cross. Then, even though corpses of crucified victims were normally thrown into anonymous graves, the Gospels state that Jesus' body was carefully laid in a new tomb belonging to a member of the Jewish Sanhedrin.

The locations for some of these events are well known: Bethany (two miles east of Jerusalem, on a ridge of the Mount of Olives), the Temple (atop the Temple Mount at the east edge of Jerusalem), and the place called Gethsemane (low on the western slope of the Mount of Olives, across from the Temple Mount[58]). But, despite assurances by modern tourist guides, the exact locations of other events are somewhat less certain. It is these locations that we will examine, keeping in mind that the primary issue is not precisely *where* the events occurred, but *whether* they occurred at all.

The ancient writings. As noted in chapter three, various ancient writings support the historical reality of Jesus' death by cru-

---

[58] Gethsemane consisted of an olive grove (described for today's tourists as the "Garden of Gethsemane") and an adjacent cave containing one or two olive presses (known today as the "Grotto of the Betrayal"). Jack Finegan, *The Archeology of the New Testament*, pp. 174–178; Joan E. Taylor, "The Garden of Gethsemane," *Biblical Archaeology Review* (July/August, 1995), pp. 26–35.

cifixion. The Roman historian Tacitus states that he was executed by Pontius Pilate, that his movement was temporarily stopped in its tracks, and that it later resurfaced in both Judea and Rome. This is consistent with the Gospels, and also with Luke's book of Acts. Similarly, the gentile writings of Thallus, Mara bar Serapion, and Lucian of Samosata constitute bits of evidence for Jesus' crucifixion. The writings of the Jewish historian Josephus provide still further support. So there is little reason to think that the essential gospel story of Jesus' death is untrue.

However, before turning to the archaeological evidence, we need to examine one other piece of Jewish writing that is often used to support the gospel accounts. Rabbinic literature of the period from A.D. 70 to 200 contains a tractate designated as *Babylonian Talmud, Sanhedrin 43a*, reading as follows:

> It has been taught: On the eve of Passover they hanged Yeshu [Jesus]. And an announcer went out, in front of him, for forty days (saying): "He is going to be stoned, because he practiced sorcery and enticed and led Israel astray. Anyone who knows anything in his favor, let him come and plead in his behalf." But, not having found anything in his favor, they hanged him on the eve of Passover.[59]

At first blush, this passage seems to confirm the story of Jesus' crucifixion. Many scholars think it does. *Yeshu* is the Hebrew version of the Greek *Jesus*, who the Gospels tell us was executed at Passover time. He performed feats that must have seemed like sorcery. From the Jewish viewpoint, he had tried to lead Israel astray. All of this is consistent with *Babylonian Talmud, Sanhedrin 43a*.

But there are countervailing arguments. According to at least one scholar, the forty-day announcement of any planned stoning (the customary form of Jewish execution) was a sort of public appeal for evidence that might exonerate the accused. Then, if the stoning actually took place, the Jews normally hung the corpse in

---

[59] Quoted from Josh McDowell & Bill Wilson, *He Walked Among Us*, p. 64.

public as a form of deterrence. If the quoted passage is describing this sort of procedure, then it could not refer to the Jesus of the Gospels, who was crucified by the Romans, not stoned by the Jews. Moreover, the gospel accounts leave no room for a forty-day period. But other scholars point out that the word *hang* is used in the New Testament as a synonym for crucifixion and that the entire idea of a forty-day period to announce an execution would have been inconsistent with Jewish criminal procedure. And so the debate surges back and forth.

Compared with the other ancient writings mentioned above, *Sanhedrin 43a* is, at best, an ambiguous piece of evidence for Jesus' crucifixion.

We will now turn to the other evidence that bears on the gospel story about Jesus' final week in Jerusalem.

The Last Supper. On the night before his death, Jesus and his disciples shared one last meal.[60] It took place in the large, upper guest room of a private home in Jerusalem. The exact location is not certain. But we do know from Epiphanius's book about Palestinian geography, written in A.D. 392, that the Roman emperor Hadrian had visited Jerusalem in A.D. 130 and had found on Mount Zion (Jerusalem's southwest hill) the small church:

> where the disciples, when they had returned after the Savior had ascended from the Mount of Olives, went to *the upper room.*[61]

In all likelihood, this small second-century church had been created out of the private home, and its upper room, where the disciples had congregated after Jesus' ascension. It was probably the same "upper room" in which the Last Supper had been held—a conclusion strengthened by comments of Origen in A.D. 230–250 and Aetheria in A.D. 381–384.[62]

---

[60] Matthew 26:17–19; Mark 14:12–15; Luke 22:7–13.
[61] Quoted by Jack Finegan, *The Archeology of the New Testament*, p. 233 (emphasis added). Reprinted by permission of Princeton University Press.
[62] Jack Finegan, *The Archeology of the New Testament*, pp. 234–235.

Today a sprawling building on Mount Zion, said to contain the tomb of King David, is supposed to be the site of the upper room where Jesus and his disciples shared their Last Supper. The room itself is sometimes called the Cenacle. Unfortunately, it is now in the form of an eleventh-century gothic chapel, thus presenting no sense of what the original room must have looked like. But the site itself could well be authentic.

Excavations have revealed that the lowest layer of flooring in the building dates from the first century A.D. Fragments of the earliest walls bear graffiti, including the name of Jesus. The building, of which the flooring and walls were part, was probably the small Judeo-Christian church that Hadrian saw in A.D. 130. Sometime around A.D. 340, the Byzantines built a bigger church over it, which was destroyed by the Arabs in A.D. 966. It was replaced by a Crusader church 133 years later, and several twelfth-century writers described the Crusader church as the site of the Last Supper. Then in 1219 it, too, was destroyed, this time by the Sultan of Damascus. But he fortunately spared the "upper room," which was eventually restored by fourteenth-century Franciscans to the form that exists today. Finally, in 1523, the rest of the building was converted into a Muslim Mosque of the Prophet David.

By tracing the history of this site back to Hadrian's visit in A.D. 130, we can be fairly confident that today's Cenacle is the actual location—although not the original structure—of the room in which the Last Supper was held.

Joseph Caiaphas. The Gospels state that, after the Last Supper, Jesus and his disciples went to Gethsemane, where he was later arrested and taken to one or more hearings before the Sanhedrin, the Jewish ruling body. The four gospels are not clear about the sequence of events, but they do contain one common thread: A hearing took place at the house of the then current high priest, whom Matthew, Luke, and John identify as Caiaphas.[63] Did this man really exist outside the minds of the gospel authors? The answer is yes.

---

[63] Matthew 26:57–68; Mark 14:53–65; Luke 3:2, 22:54; John 18:12–24.

Caiaphas appears to have held the position of high priest from A.D. 18 to 36. Josephus provides the first piece of confirming evidence, writing about "Joseph, who was called Caiaphas, of the high priesthood."[64] The second piece of confirming evidence was discovered in late 1990. Inside a cave, just south of Jerusalem, archaeologists discovered twelve stone ossuaries (receptacles for the reburied bones of dead people after their flesh had decomposed).[65] The Jewish tomb in which they were found dates from around the time of Jesus, as evidenced by the presence of a coin minted by Herod Agrippa between A.D. 37 and 44 and by the fact that Jews seldom used ossuaries after Jerusalem was destroyed in A.D. 70. On one ossuary, which had elegant carving on the front side, the name "Joseph son of Caiaphas" had been incised on one end and on the back side. It contained the bones of a sixty-year old man, a woman, and four children. The word *Caiaphas* was probably an informal family name, and "Joseph" was the particular man whose bones were interred in the ossuary. This is the first archaeological evidence that the Caiaphas of the Gospels really existed.

What about the location of his house in Jerusalem, where Jesus was interrogated? Archaeology has perhaps uncovered it. According to Josephus, revolutionists went into Jerusalem's upper city (Mount Zion) in A.D. 66. They burned the palaces of Herod Agrippa and his sister Bernice (the locations have probably been identified), as well as the house of the high priest at that time (which was probably located close by the palaces).[66] This may have been a house used by a whole succession of high priests, including Joseph Caiaphas some thirty-five years earlier. Even if it was not, Joseph's house must have been nearby. When the Bordeaux Pilgrim came to Jerusalem in A.D. 333, he was taken up to this area and shown where Caiaphas's house had once been. Then in A.D.

---

[64] Josephus, "Antiquities of the Jews" 18.95, *The Works*, p. 483.

[65] Zvi Greenhut, "Burial Cave of the Caiaphas Family," *Biblical Archaeology Review* (September/October, 1992), pp. 28–36; Ronny Reich, "Caiaphas Name Inscribed on Bone Boxes," Ibid., pp. 38–44.

[66] Josephus, "Wars of the Jews" 2.426, *The Works*, p. 625.

530 Theodosius wrote that a church in honor of Peter (who had denied Jesus three times in Caiaphas's courtyard) had been built at the site of Caiaphas's house and that it was located about fifty paces from the Church of Holy Zion (the church which had been built at the site of the Last Supper). Unfortunately, Theodosius does not give any particular direction. However, excavations at the present Armenian Monastery of Saint Savior (claimed to have been built around the house of Caiaphas), which lies fifty meters north of the Cenacle, have revealed a sixth-century church, which probably was the Church of Peter described by Theodosius. It is likely the authentic site of Caiaphas's house, especially since other excavations in the area have revealed the presence of luxurious homes from the Herodian period.

The only rival site is the modern Church of Saint Peter in Gallicantu, which commemorates Peter's weeping after the cock crowed and reminded him that he had denied Jesus three times. Archaeological excavations have revealed that this site was venerated as early as the fifth century. Subsequent writers from the eighth through the twelfth centuries identified a commemorative church at that location. However, this is probably not the site of Caiaphas's house. It lies nearly three hundred yards from the Cenacle—far more than Theodosius's fifty paces. Moreover, it is on the direct path from the Last Supper to Gethsemane. Jesus would have been taking an extraordinary risk to lead his followers right alongside Caiaphas's house on that high-stakes evening.

To summarize, we can be confident that Caiaphas was a real high priest who played a real role in Jesus' death. We can also make an informed judgment about the location of his house, where Jesus underwent a hearing that led him to Pilate and to crucifixion.

Pontius Pilate. Most people know that Pilate was the Roman governor who interrogated Jesus and then ordered him to be crucified. But many are not aware of how much information is available about this man. It is, in fact, quite abundant, providing extensive background support for the gospel portraits of him and of his pivotal role in Christianity's crucial event.

Pilate served as governor of Judea for about ten years, beginning in A.D. 26. The earliest existing reference to him comes from the pen of Philo, a Jewish philosopher in Alexandria, who lived from around 20 B.C. to about A.D. 50—the very period during which Pilate had his encounter with Jesus.[67] Philo describes a letter written by Herod Agrippa I (grandson of Herod the Great) to the emperor Caligula in A.D. 40. In it Herod Agrippa characterizes Pilate as "naturally inflexible, a blend of self-will and relentlessness."[68] He then relates an episode several years earlier, when Pilate had hung in Herod's Jerusalem palace some gilded shields dedicated to the emperor Tiberius. This act was so offensive to Jewish leaders that all four of Herod the Great's sons appealed the matter to Tiberius. The emperor ordered Pilate to remove the shields.

A similar example of Pilate's insensitivity to Jewish traditions is described by Josephus in his extensive account of Pilate's governorship. During a winter night, Pilate ordered images of the emperor introduced into Jerusalem. It was the first time a governor had done this, and the Jews were so incensed that multitudes of them went down to Pilate's headquarters in Caesarea. After a major confrontation, Pilate backed down and had the images removed from Jerusalem and brought to Caesarea.[69]

These two reports of Pilate's behavior help clarify Mark's comment that the governor's purpose in setting Barabbas free and ordering Jesus crucified was "to satisfy the crowd."[70] Pilate simply did not want any more trouble with the Jews because he knew the emperor might be angered if he learned that Pilate had once again fomented a dispute with them.

From the pages of Philo and Josephus, supplemented by Tacitus's brief reference noted earlier in this chapter, the Pilate described in the Gospels seems to have been a real man who actually

---

[67] Described by E. M. Blaiklock, *The Archaeology of the New Testament* (Grand Rapids, MI: Zondervan, 1970), p. 67.

[68] Quoted by F. F. Bruce, *New Testament History*, p. 34.

[69] Josephus, "Antiquities of the Jews" 18.55–59, *The Works*, pp. 479–480.

[70] Mark 15:15. Luke's account is similar (23:23–25).

served as governor of Judea at the time of Jesus' crucifixion. In 1961 this literary evidence was archaeologically corroborated by the discovery of a two-foot-by-three-foot stone slab at the Roman theater in Caesarea. It is now housed at the Israel Museum in Jerusalem. The left side has been chipped off, but the remaining right side bears three lines of a Latin inscription, the middle one reading "TIVSPILATVS." When combined with the surviving words of the other two lines, the entire original inscription (translated from Latin to English) probably read as follows:

> Pontius Pilate, Prefect of Judea, has presented the Tiberium [evidently a temple dedicated to the emperor] to the Caesareans.[71]

One other question remains: Where did Pilate's interrogation of Jesus take place? The answer is that we don't really know. The Gospels merely state that it occurred at the place which Pilate used as his headquarters whenever he journeyed from Caesarea to Jerusalem.

Three locations are plausible sites for his Jerusalem headquarters. First is the Fortress Antonia, built by Herod the Great in honor of his friend Marc Antony, at the northwest corner of the Temple Mount. This is the place where today's tourists, after a look at paving stones on which Roman soldiers allegedly gambled, start walking along the Via Dolorosa (Way of Sorrows) to the traditional site of Jesus' crucifixion. The second possible location is the old Hasmonean palace that Herod the Great took over when he became king. Southwest of the Temple Mount, it is commonly called the Lower Palace. The third possibility is the lavish palace that Herod the Great built for himself at the western edge of Jerusalem, commonly called the Upper Palace.

Nothing remains of the structures that once stood at these three locations. But the Fortress Antonia is the least likely candidate for Pilate's headquarters, since it was basically a military barracks, not a sumptuous governor's residence. As between the two Herodian

---

[71] Quoted by Josh McDowell & Bill Wilson, *He Walked Among Us*, p. 215.

palaces, there is little to choose. The existing evidence goes both ways. So the most we can say is that Jesus' interrogation by Pilate took place somewhere in Jerusalem.

The nature of crucifixion. Before looking at the place where Jesus was crucified, we should take a brief look at the grisly process itself.

Modern representations of the cross tend to be quite sanitized. They seldom capture the prolonged and bloody brutality of this ancient form of capital punishment. So whenever the word *crucifixion* is used, we should clearly understand that crucified victims, including Jesus, were physically brutalized to an extent that is hard to comprehend today.

Crucifixion had been practiced by eastern cultures, like the Assyrians and the Persians, for many centuries before the time of Jesus. Alexander the Great brought it west to places like Carthage, from which the Romans evidently learned it. Within the Roman Empire, tens of thousands of people were crucified. But not until 1968 were the remains of a crucified victim actually discovered. It occurred during excavations for a new housing project northeast of Jerusalem. In the tomb of a moderately wealthy Jewish family, eight ossuaries were found containing the bones of seventeen people. One of them, a man between twenty-four and twenty-eight years old, had been crucified.[72] He was five feet six inches tall, and his name was "Yehohanan, the son of Hagakol." His heel bone was attached to the vertical post of the cross by means of a spike, and a piece of the wood still remained stuck to the spike's bent tip. The lower leg bones had been fractured, perhaps by a sharp blow, just like the legs of the two men who were crucified alongside Jesus.[73] This would have hastened his death and allowed for burial before

---

[72] Vassilios Tzaferis, "Crucifixion—The Archaeological Evidence," *Biblical Archaeological Review* (January/February, 1985), pp. 44–53. For an updated analysis of the man's bones and the position of his body on the cross, see Ian Wilson, *The Blood and the Shroud* (New York: The Free Press, 1998), pp. 41–53.

[73] John 19:32–33. Jesus' legs were not similarly broken, because he was already dead.

nightfall, in line with Jewish custom. A scratch on the radius bone of the right forearm, just above the wrist, indicates that his arms had been nailed (not merely tied) to the horizontal bar of the cross.

Yehohanan's crucifixion was conducted just about as we would have expected, based on the gospel accounts of Jesus and the two men who were executed beside him.

The place of Jesus' crucifixion. The traditional—and probably the true—site of Jesus' crucifixion is the place where the Church of the Holy Sepulcher stands today in the northwest quadrant of Jerusalem's Old City. Unfortunately, the succession of churches built on top of this place over the centuries has deprived modern visitors of any chance to glimpse the ancient atmosphere in which Jesus' execution was carried out. To catch such a glimpse, visitors must go to the so-called "Garden Tomb," several hundred yards away, which some Christians consider to be the true site. The Garden Tomb area reveals a small rocky hill and a normal Jewish tomb from the first century A.D. It gives a good sense of what the place of crucifixion must have looked like two thousand years ago, even though it is probably not the actual site.

According to the Gospels, Jesus was crucified at a place called Golgotha, the Aramaic word for *skull*.[74] In Latin it is translated *calva*, from which we get the English word *calvary*. It was "near the city"[75] and "outside the city gate."[76] These were accurate descriptions of the site in Jesus' day, although a few years after his death the city walls were realigned so as to put the site within the enlarged city. The place of crucifixion had a garden and a new tomb.[77]

In evaluating the authenticity of the traditional site, one important consideration should be kept in mind: The early Jerusalem Christians would undoubtedly have preserved a memory of

---

[74] Matthew 27:33; Mark 15:22; Luke 23:33.

[75] John 19:20.

[76] Hebrews 13:12.

[77] John 19:41.

the location where Jesus was crucified and buried.[78] This would have been true even after the emperor Hadrian, in A.D. 135, had excluded all Jews (including Jewish Christians) from Jerusalem. Eusebius points out that, after Hadrian's exclusion order, the city's Christian church became composed of Gentiles, and he identifies a man named Mark as Jerusalem's first gentile bishop.[79] So the expulsion of the Jews from Jerusalem would not have erased the collective Christian memory of the important Christian sites.

Based upon studies at the Church of the Holy Sepulcher, we know that this rocky area was used as a quarry from the seventh century B.C. to the first century B.C. It was then abandoned, and the site was filled with soil. It became a garden and was also used for tombs.

Two fourth-century Christian writers, Eusebius and Jerome, tell us that in about A.D. 130 the emperor Hadrian built a shrine to Venus on the rock where Jesus had been crucified.[80] Eusebius locates it in the general area of today's Church of the Holy Sepulcher, and this was confirmed by the Bordeaux Pilgrim when he visited Jerusalem in A.D. 333. At that time the emperor Constantine was having Venus's shrine cleared away so he could construct a large basilica, which was dedicated two years later. In the course of clearing the site, the rocky outcropping of Golgotha emerged. It was incorporated into the western atrium of Constantine's basilica and still stands today, sixteen feet high, inside the entrance to the Church of the Holy Sepulcher.

While delivering a series of twenty-four lectures at Constantine's basilica in A.D. 348, Cyril, Bishop of Jerusalem, referred several times to the hill "standing above us," drawing his audience's atten-

---

[78] Just before the start of the Jewish war against the Romans in A.D. 66, the Jewish Christians in Jerusalem fled to the town of Pella. Since it was only fifty miles away, their memories of Jerusalem's sites would hardly have faded. Eusebius, *The History of the Church* 3.5, p. 68.

[79] Ibid. 4.6, p. 108.

[80] Jack Finegan, *The Archeology of the New Testament*, pp. 261–262.

tion to the fact that Jesus was crucified "on Golgotha *here*."[81] He also mentioned that Jesus' nearby tomb had once been a garden, just as the Gospel of John describes. Having been born in Jerusalem around A.D. 315, Cyril would have been familiar with the traditional location of Golgotha and the tomb, even before Constantine started to construct his new basilica on the site.

So a fair amount of evidence supports the Church of the Holy Sepulcher as the true site of Jesus' crucifixion.

Jesus' tomb. The Bordeaux Pilgrim, visiting Jerusalem in A.D. 333, wrote that Jesus' tomb, which had allegedly been identified six or seven years earlier, was "about a stone's throw" from Golgotha.[82] Like Golgotha, the tomb was included within Constantine's basilica complex, which, during ensuing centuries, was destroyed and rebuilt several times. The present Church of the Holy Sepulcher, a much smaller structure than Constantine's original complex, was completed by the Crusaders in 1149 and substantially repaired in 1810, following a fire two years earlier. Jesus' tomb and Golgotha are focal points of the church. They are fifty yards apart, consistent with the Bordeaux Pilgrim's "stone's throw."

Evidence for the authenticity of the precise site of Jesus' tomb within the Church of the Holy Sepulcher is fairly slim. But we do know that below ground, in the area near the small and ornate structure that contains the sepulcher itself, many ancient Jewish tombs have been discovered. Several of them, below the Chapel of the Copts, can be visited today. So there is no good reason to doubt that Jesus was actually buried in today's Holy Sepulcher, or at least in another tomb very close by.

---

[81] Ibid. pp. 266–267 (emphasis added). These lectures were published from shorthand notes taken by a member of Cyril's audience. Ibid. pp. xvii.
[82] Ibid., pp. 262–263.

From Skeptic to Christian

CONCLUSION

When all the pieces of evidence supporting the gospel accounts are assembled and reviewed, one reasonable conclusion can be drawn: In their accounts of Jesus' birth, life, and death, the gospel authors stand tall as careful writers who accurately reported real places, real people, and real events.

Now, before turning to the evidence for Jesus' alleged resurrection—the capstone of the gospel story—we need to make a brief detour into the evidence relating to Luke's book of Acts.

Chapter Six

✝

EXTERNAL EVIDENCE CORROBORATING LUKE'S BOOK OF ACTS

Luke's book of Acts recounts the early Christian movement's first thirty-five years of growth. It chronicles the activities of the disciples as they proclaim their message in and around Jerusalem. It also records the missionary journeys of Paul, a converted Jew who spent most of his last thirty years evangelizing Gentiles in the area of modern Turkey and Greece. The book ends abruptly, with Paul as a prisoner in Rome awaiting trial before the emperor Nero.

In reality, Acts is a continuation of Luke's gospel. It picks up where the gospel story ends, with Jesus' resurrection and subsequent ascension to heaven. Together, Luke's gospel and Acts effectively form a single work.

Like the four gospels, the book of Acts can be subjected to a search for external corroborating evidence. If it turns out that Acts is an accurate historical account, then the historical truth of Luke's *gospel* automatically becomes more probable. This is true because an historian who is habitually trustworthy in the second half of his book can be presumed equally trustworthy in the first half.

LITERARY EVIDENCE

Felix. Luke refers to a man named Felix, identifying him as the governor of Judea who interrogated the apostle Paul. At that time Paul was on his way to Rome for trial on charges brought by the Jewish leaders in Jerusalem. According to Luke, Felix gave Paul a hearing, talked with him frequently, but did not make a decision in the case. Luke mentions that Felix's wife was named Drusilla.[1]

Felix's historical existence, as an actual person who governed Judea and as the husband of Drusilla, is confirmed by Tacitus, Suetonius, and Josephus. Tacitus identifies him as a freedman of the emperor Claudius and as having been entrusted with the province of Judea. Tacitus colorfully depicts him as a man who, indulging:

> in every kind of barbarity and lust, exercised the power of a king in the spirit of a slave. He had married Drusilla, the granddaughter of Antony and Cleopatra.[2]

Suetonius corroborates Tacitus's identification of Felix. Although not mentioning that Felix had a wife named Drusilla, Suetonius does comment that he married three queens.[3]

Josephus chronicles many details of Felix's career, including specific confirmation that he had received his position from Claudius and had married a woman named Drusilla.[4]

Festus. Luke tells us that Festus was Felix's successor and that he too gave Paul a hearing. But the hearing was quite brief because Paul, exercising his right as a Roman citizen, appealed the case directly to the emperor (Nero at that time).[5] Festus's position as successor to Felix is verified by Josephus, who relates various events of his governorship, right up to his death.[6]

Judas the Galilean. According to Luke, the Pharisee Gamaliel once reminded the Sanhedrin that this Judas had:

---

[1] Acts 24.

[2] Tacitus, *Histories* 5.9, p. 297; see also Tacitus, *Annals* 12.54, p. 122. Reprinted from *Great Books of the Western World* © 1952, 1990 Encyclopaedia Britannica, Inc.

[3] Suetonius, "Claudius" 28, *The Twelve Caesars*, p. 204.

[4] "Antiquities of the Jews" 20.137–143, *The Works*, pp. 533–534.

[5] Acts 25:1–12.

[6] "Antiquities of the Jews" 20.182–197, *The Works*, pp. 536–537.

appeared in the days of the census and led a band of people in revolt.[7]

Josephus records the same event. Writing about the Jews who had capitulated to the Roman taxation census, he comments that this Judas:

> became zealous to draw them to a revolt. . .and exhorted the nation to assert their liberty.[8]

The Egyptian. Luke tells us that Paul had been mistakenly identified by a Roman commander as the Egyptian leader of a revolt at some earlier time.[9] The same man, and his revolt, is also described by Josephus.[10]

Expulsion of Jews from Rome. Luke states, "Claudius had ordered all the Jews to leave Rome."[11] Suetonius confirms this statement in his biography of Claudius (who was emperor from A.D. 41 to 54), commenting that:

> because the Jews at Rome caused continuous disturbances at the instigation of Chrestus [Christ], he [Claudius] expelled them from the city.[12]

The most plausible explanation for the expulsion, which probably occurred around A.D. 49, is that conflicts had arisen between the Jews and their new offshoot group, the Christians. In Claudius's mind the difference between the two groups would not have been noticeable. They were all "Jews." Some of them had been

---

[7] Acts 5:37.

[8] "Antiquities of the Jews" 18.4, *The Works,* p. 476.

[9] Acts 21:37–39.

[10] "Antiquities of the Jews" 20.169–172, *The Works,* p. 536.

[11] Acts 18:1–2.

[12] Suetonius, "Claudius" 25, *The Twelve Caesars,* trans. Robert Graves, rev. ed. (London: Penguin Group, 1979), p. 202. Reprinted by permission of Carcanet Press Limited.

instigated by "Chrestus" to cause disturbances. Some had not. So he simply expelled them all.

Death of Herod Agrippa I. King Herod Agrippa I, grandson of Herod the Great, reigned over Judea from A.D. 37 to 44. Luke writes that he imprisoned the disciple Peter and ordered the death of the disciple James (the brother of John).[13] Here is Luke's graphic account of Agrippa's death:

> Then Herod [Agrippa] went from Judea to Caesarea and stayed there a while. He had been quarreling with the people of Tyre and Sidon. . .On the appointed day [for a peace audience with them] Herod, wearing his royal robes, sat on his throne and delivered a public address to the people. They shouted, "This is the voice of a god, not of a man." Immediately, because Herod did not give praise to God, an angel of the Lord struck him down, and he was eaten by worms and died.[14]

Josephus's equally graphic description of the same event bears a startling similarity to Luke's report:

> Now, when Agrippa had reigned three years over all Judea, he came to the city Cesarea. . .[H]e put on a garment made wholly of silver, and of a contexture truly wonderful, and came into the theatre early in the morning; at which time the silver of his garment being illuminated by the fresh reflection of the sun's rays upon it, shone out after a surprising manner. . .and presently his flatterers cried out. . .that he was a god. . .Upon this the king did neither rebuke them, nor reject their impious flattery. But, as he presently afterwards looked up, he saw an owl sitting on a certain rope over his head, and immediately understood that this bird was the messenger of ill tidings. . .and [he] fell into the deepest sorrow. A severe pain also arose in his belly. . .And when he had been quite worn out by the pain in his belly for five days, he departed this life, being in the fifty-fourth year of his age.[15]

---

[13] Acts 12:2–4.
[14] Acts 12:19–23.
[15] "Antiquities of the Jews" 19.343–350, *The Works*, pp. 523–524.

Beyond doubt, Josephus and Luke are telling the same story, with many of the same details. It provides a vivid example of the extent to which Josephus, with no ax to grind on behalf of the Christians, corroborates Luke's veracity.

ARCHAEOLOGICAL EVIDENCE

Luke exhibits a detailed knowledge of geography around the Mediterranean area, correctly identifying numerous countries, cities, and islands. Even more impressively, he displays thorough familiarity with the many different titles used for official positions throughout the Roman Empire. This was not as simple as it may seem today. Nearly two thousand years later we are accustomed to countless reference sources. We have vast libraries and computer networks. But Luke had no such centralized sources. He had to ferret out the official titles one by one. His work was made more difficult by the fact that titles were not uniform throughout the empire and that they sometimes changed. Archaeological evidence reveals that, remarkably, Luke seems to have gotten them right every time.

Gallio of Achaia. Luke refers to a man named Gallio as "proconsul" of Achaia (the southern portion of modern Greece).[16] Various Roman writings, including those of Tacitus, mention Junius Gallio. He was the brother of Seneca, the Roman philosopher who served as Nero's tutor, and he was executed by Nero in A.D. 65. An inscription, probably from the emperor Claudius, has been found at Delphi, about seventy-five miles northwest of Athens. It confirms that Gallio did indeed hold the position of Achaia's proconsul, beginning in A.D. 51.

Ephesus. An ancient Greek city, Ephesus was located on the west coast of modern Turkey. Luke describes a riot that broke out there, instigated by silversmiths whose income from selling statues of the goddess Artemis was being eroded by the increasing

---

[16] Acts 18:12–17.

number of Christians. He reports that the *grammateus* (city clerk) quieted the crowd by reminding them that Ephesus was the *neokoros* (servant or guardian) of the temple of Artemis.[17] Application of these two Greek terms to the city of Ephesus has been confirmed by inscriptional evidence.[18]

In addition, Luke's mention of the silversmiths finds circumstantial support from an inscription that has been discovered at the theater in Ephesus. Dated to A.D. 103/104, it identifies a Roman official who presented several silver statues, including one of Artemis, to be displayed in the theater at each meeting of the populace.[19]

Politarchs of Thessalonica. Luke tells us that Paul became the focal point of turmoil in Thessalonica and that the city's *politarchs* were involved.[20] This Greek word, typically translated today as "officials" or "authorities," is found nowhere else in ancient classical literature. So early scholars were unsure about its use by Luke. But in 1835 this very word was discovered in a Greek inscription on an arch spanning a street on the west side of Thessalonica. Since then, many other inscriptions have been found bearing the same title, thus vindicating Luke's use of the unusual Greek word.[21]

Chief official of Malta. Luke reports that Paul and his companions, on their way to Rome, were shipwrecked on the island of Malta.[22] Because Luke uses the words *we* and *us*, he himself was likely one of the group. The stranded party was welcomed by the

---

[17] Acts 19:23–41. The city clerk was the chief local official, acting as liaison to the Romans. The term "guardian" of the temple was a title of honor bestowed on the whole city.

[18] *New Bible Dictionary*, 2d ed. (Wheaton, IL: Tyndale House, 1982), p. 337; F. F. Bruce, *The New Testament Documents*, p. 84.

[19] F. F. Bruce, *The New Testament Documents*, p. 84.

[20] Acts 17:6.

[21] E. M. Blaiklock, *The Archaeology of the New Testament*, pp. 97–99; John McRay, *Archaeology and the New Testament* (Grand Rapids, MI: Baker Book House, 1991), p. 295; Study Note to Acts 17:6, *The NIV Study Bible* (Grand Rapids, MI: Zondervan, 1985), p. 1679.

[22] Acts 27:27–28:10.

inhabitants and by Publius, the *protos* of the island. This Greek word is translated "chief man" in the King James Version, and "chief official" in the NIV. Inscriptional evidence in both Greek and Latin has revealed that it was the correct title for the person who served as Rome's governor of Malta.[23]

Areopagus of Athens. Luke tells us that, in Athens, Paul was brought to "a meeting of the Areopagus."[24] This rocky hill near the Acropolis had been well known for many centuries before Jesus' time as the sacred meeting place of the Athenian council of elders. In fact, at an early date the council itself took on the name of the hill, retaining it even after the meeting location was moved to the colonnaded structure beside the city's marketplace. By the first century A.D., the council had lost some of its former stature, but it still kept its religious characteristics. Just as Luke reports, it was the very group to which Paul would have been expected to pro-claim his ideas about Jesus and the resurrection.

Lystra. Luke describes the visit of Paul and Barnabas to the city of Lystra (in the south-central part of modern Turkey). After Paul had healed a crippled man, the populace began to call him and Barnabas by the names of "Zeus" (the Greek name for the Roman god Jupiter) and "Hermes" (the Greek name for the Roman god Mercury).[25] In the late nineteenth century an old inscription was discovered at Lystra. It dedicated a statue to Zeus and Hermes, who were evidently linked with the city. So the reaction that Luke reported is consistent with what we would expect from this city's people when they became excited about Paul and Barnabas.[26]

Erastus of Corinth. Before concluding, we should look at the archaeological evidence bearing on references by Luke, and also by Paul, to a man called Erastus. It may or may not have been a common name in the first century A.D.

---

[23] F. F. Bruce, *The New Testament Documents*, p. 85.
[24] Acts 17:19.
[25] Acts 14:8–12.
[26] E. M. Blaiklock, *The Archaeology of the New Testament*, p. 96.

Erastus is mentioned three times in the New Testament, and he is likely the same person on each occasion. We first meet him in Luke's book of Acts. Paul is on a third missionary journey sometime between A.D. 53 and 57. He has traveled overland from Antioch to Ephesus, where he decides to remain for a while. So he sends his two helpers on to Macedonia. One of them is Erastus.[27] We next hear about Erastus in Paul's letter to the Roman Christians, written around A.D. 57 from in or near the Greek city of Corinth. He concludes the letter by sending greetings from various companions, including "Erastus, who is the city's director of public works."[28] Several years later, near the end of his life, Paul wrote to his friend Timothy. In the letter he mentions, "Erastus stayed in Corinth."[29]

For many centuries Erastus was just a name. But in 1929 an American archaeological expedition in Corinth discovered a marble slab, part of a pavement near the city theater, dated to the first century A.D. On it was the following Latin inscription:

> Erastus, in consideration of his appointment as curator of buildings, laid this pavement at his own expense.[30]

This is virtually identical to Paul's description of Erastus's position. Even if the name had been a common one, we can be fairly certain that the Erastus on the marble slab was the same man identified by Paul in his letter to the Romans.[31] Then, when the other two references to Erastus (in Acts and Timothy) are examined in the contexts of chronology and geography, it is reasonable to conclude that they too are referring to him. So archaeology seems to

---

[27] Acts 19:22.

[28] Romans 16:23.

[29] 2 Timothy 4:20.

[30] Quoted by F. F. Bruce, *Jesus and Christian Origins Outside the New Testament*, p. 200. Reproduced by permission of Hodder and Stoughton Limited and William Neill-Hall Ltd.

[31] John McRay, *Archaeology and the New Testament*, pp. 331–332.

have confirmed the identity of an obscure person who is mentioned three times, ever so briefly, in the New Testament pages.

Conclusion

In chapter five and in this chapter we have reviewed many factual details from the Gospels and the book of Acts. These details are corroborated by ancient manuscripts, by astronomical events, and by archaeological discoveries. A few of the conclusions are debatable, but most of them are solid. The evidence indeed supports the historical authenticity of many people, places, and events appearing on the gospel tapestry.

Numerous evidentiary gaps do remain, like the lack of independent corroboration for the gospel record of the things Jesus purportedly said and taught. Skeptics can certainly dispute the reliability of all these gospel statements for which we have no evidence one way or the other. But in doing so they must jettison the face value presumption of historical accuracy. And in its place they must adopt a curious assumption: Four different authors, whose statements always proved to be *correct* when they could be tested by evidence, are *wrong* in most of their statements for which evidentiary testing is not yet available. Skeptics face an awesome task in making sense out of such an idea.

Chapter Seven

✝

EVIDENCE CORROBORATING JESUS' RESURRECTION

INTRODUCTION

As described in Chapter four, the New Testament gospels trace their lineages directly back to ancient manuscript sources. Their stories about Jesus' birth, life, and death lead most people, even the most zealous atheists, to concede that he was a fascinating historical figure. But history is replete with fascinating figures. What was so special about this one? The standard Christian response is that Jesus claimed he and God were one and the same. Yet anybody—even today—can make such a claim. So the question still remains: Why should anyone be persuaded that Jesus was uniquely different?

The answer, according to the Gospels, is that he was resurrected bodily from the dead.[1] This is an extraordinary assertion—one that is celebrated every year on Easter Sunday, when a dynamic delivery of the preacher's message can even touch the hearts of dedicated skeptics. However, on the way home they will likely revert to their bedrock belief that the resurrection of Jesus, as an historical event, could not really have happened. It would be just too "supernatural" for practical and rational people to accept.

---

[1] The gospels describe something more than just the *resuscitation* of an apparently dead person back to consciousness, since that person will eventually die. They also describe something more than the resurrection of a person into a new *spiritual* form.

Yet, despite such intellectual skepticism, the claimed historical truth of this very event remains at the center of the Christian faith. And a good deal of evidence bears on its plausibility.

Jesus' alleged resurrection is based upon the gospel descriptions of observable facts. These descriptions can be taken at face value, unless there is good reason to dispute them. In other words, reports of claimed facts like the empty tomb and Jesus' post-crucifixion appearances can be presumed accurate unless there is reason to think that the gospel writers lied, exaggerated, utilized inadequate evidence, or were writing metaphor, allegory, fiction, or legend. Without some such reason, the "facts" reported in the Gospels deserve face value credibility.

The pivotal point is that everyone—whether atheist, agnostic, or non-Christian believer in the existence of a God—needs to form an opinion one way or the other about the historical reality of Jesus' resurrection. As the apostle Paul passionately pointed out:

> if Christ has not been raised [resurrected], our preaching is *useless* and so is your faith. . .[I]f Christ has not been raised, your faith is *futile*.[2]

If God did indeed resurrect Jesus from the death he had suffered on a Roman cross—if it was an actual historical event in time and space—then we appear to have powerful support for two conclusions: First, God exists (since nobody else is capable of orchestrating such a supernatural episode). Second, Jesus, who claimed to be God, was more than just another human being (since God doesn't seem to have resurrected anybody else in recorded history).

Not everyone accepts the logic of these two conclusions. For example, one atheist philosopher has commented that if Jesus' resurrection actually happened:

> it wouldn't give you any way of being able to detect if there is a God. It would be just that a very strange happening happened

---

[2] 1 Corinthians 15:14–17 (emphasis added).

. . .a very peculiar fact we hadn't explained and indeed lacked the scientific resources to explain.[3]

I suspect that most skeptical people (including myself many years ago) would dispute this point of view. If they were somehow convinced that Jesus really did rise from the dead, they would probably concede the likelihood that a supernatural God exists and that, for some reason, he was uniquely fond of Jesus.

THE CLAIMED RESURRECTION EVENT

The evidence for the resurrection needs to be put into the context of the post-crucifixion events as described in the Gospels.[4] These alleged events can be summarized as follows:

Jesus died on the cross, as confirmed by a Roman spear thrust into his side. Then a wealthy member of the Jewish ruling council, Joseph of Arimathea, after obtaining permission from the Roman governor Pilate, placed the body in his own new tomb, sealing it with a large stone.[5] It was late on an afternoon, probably Friday, and two of Jesus' female disciples watched from nearby. On Saturday, the Jewish Sabbath, a guard was posted at the tomb. Early on Sunday morning the women returned to the tomb and found it empty. A young man in white clothing told them that Jesus had risen. They immediately reported to the disciples. Peter and John ran to the tomb, confirming that Jesus' body was gone and that nothing remained except the linen in

---

[3] J. P. Moreland and Kai Nielsen, *Does God Exist?*, p. 64.
[4] Matthew 27:57–28:20; Mark 15:42–16:20 (although verses 9–20 do not appear in the oldest manuscripts); Luke 23:50–24:49; John 19:38–20:25.
[5] The notion that Jesus was buried in a wealthy man's private tomb has sometimes been dismissed as a legend. The argument is that Jesus' body was pitched into the sort of unmarked, mass grave that was typically used for crucified victims. However, the 1968 discovery of a crucified man's bones in an ossuary within a private tomb virtually destroys this argument. See pp. 108–109.

which the corpse had been wrapped. (The gospel authors failed to describe the resurrection event itself—a detail that would have been irresistible if they had been writing fiction.) During the ensuing days and weeks, on various occasions and in various places, the risen Jesus appeared to his disciples and to others.

That's the story, and, just as with the reconstruction of any other ancient event, nobody can conclude with one hundred percent certainty that it actually happened. But everybody can—and should—examine the known facts and then decide for himself or herself whether the New Testament accounts provide the best explanation for them.

The Emptiness of the Tomb

The starting point of the Gospels' resurrection story is the arrival of several women at Jesus' tomb early on the second morning after his crucifixion.[6] Their purpose was to anoint the body with spices, evidently because the Jewish burial procedures had been interrupted by the start of the Sabbath at dusk two days earlier. Upon arrival, they found that the stone seal had been rolled away and that the body was nowhere to be found. The tomb was empty.

This is a description of observable events. Even without corroborating evidence, it deserves the face value presumption of historical accuracy. And its credibility is enhanced by the differences among the four gospel accounts of the empty tomb. They vary from each other in several details, and they display a few dangling loose ends—just enough to permeate the entire story with a ring of reliability.[7]

Admittedly the empty tomb, standing alone, does not prove that Jesus was resurrected from the dead. But it does constitute the first component of the resurrection evidence. And several lines of argument support it.

---

[6] Matthew 28:1–6; Mark 16:1–6; Luke 24:1–6; John 20:1–2.
[7] See pp. 66–71.

A fraud would have been exposed. The disciples' public proclamation of the resurrection commenced just seven weeks after the crucifixion.[8] If Jesus' body had still been inside the tomb, their claim that he had been raised from the dead would have been quickly exposed as a fraud. But no such disproof was ever recorded. Various anti-resurrection arguments were advanced to *explain* the empty tomb (as will be noted shortly), but none was offered to *dispute* it. While arguments from silence are seldom powerful, this one tends to be an exception. If the tomb had not really been empty, then the early critics who sought to explain it away would have publicly removed Jesus' decaying body and displayed it as conclusive proof that the claimed resurrection was a hoax. Christianity would have been stopped in its tracks. But no such thing happened. Instead, the critics' inability to produce Jesus' body forced them to retreat into explanations for *why* the tomb was empty. This retreat, standing alone, is evidence that the tomb did not contain a body.

Furthermore, four distinct lines of logic neutralize any contention that the empty tomb story was a fraud and that Jesus' body remained inside for weeks or months after the crucifixion. Each line of logic takes into account the behavior of various people in the New Testament drama—behavior which would have been inconsistent with a tomb that still contained a body.

First, according to Luke's book of Acts, Peter and the other disciples began to preach about Jesus' resurrection just a few weeks after his crucifixion and entombment. They did so right in Jerusalem, the very city where everything had occurred. Would the disciples have been so foolish as to proclaim that Jesus was raised from the dead if any listener could have made the short walk to Golgotha, peered into the nearby tomb, and come face to face with Jesus' decomposed body? Of course not. The disciples may have been uneducated, and perhaps even misguided, but they could hardly have been stupid. They would not have knowingly

---

[8] Acts 2.

proclaimed a false message right next door to the very evidence that would unmask their duplicity. Instead, they would have gone far away, probably a hundred miles to the north in their native Galilee, where the risk of exposure would have been far less.

Second, if Jesus' body had still been in the tomb, either the Jewish authorities, or the Roman authorities, or both, would have exposed and publicized the Christian resurrection claim as a hoax. The Jews would have done so because of the bedrock Christian assertion that the resurrected Jesus was their long-awaited Jewish messiah. The Romans would have done so because a religious conflict between the Christians and the Jews would create a risk of civil unrest. The best way for both Jewish and Roman authorities to squelch the Christian resurrection message would have been to produce Jesus' body. But nobody did.

Third, an educated rabbi like Saul of Tarsus, who converted from an ardent persecutor of Christians to a believer in their faith, would not have remained a lifelong convert if he had doubted Peter's and John's claim that the tomb was empty on Easter morning. Yet Saul remained steadfast. Far from reneging on his conversion, which had occurred just a few years after Jesus' crucifixion, he became the apostle Paul, an indefatigable missionary traveler who spent the rest of his life spreading the Christian gospel throughout much of the Mediterranean world. He made various visits to Jerusalem, starting with the two weeks he spent there with Peter about three years after his conversion.[9] If Jesus' nearby tomb had not already been well known as empty, Paul would hardly have remained convinced that the resurrection was a true historical event.

Fourth, if the tomb had not been empty, the disciples would have been risking their lives for a claim they knew to be false. Most of these men did indeed suffer martyrdom for their faith. It would have defied human nature for them to do so *knowingly* (as distinct from unwittingly). By putting their lives on the line, they were testifying eloquently to their own firm conviction that Jesus' tomb was empty.

---

[9] Galatians 1:18.

The Nazareth Decree confirms the controversy. A formidable piece of circumstantial evidence for the emptiness of Jesus' tomb comes from the hardheaded world of archaeology. It consists of an obscure Greek inscription on a fifteen-by-twenty-four-inch marble slab that, in 1878, was sent from Nazareth to a Parisian archaeologist. Upon his death, the slab was transferred to the Louvre, where it was finally examined in 1930, turning out to be a rather poor Greek translation from a Latin original. Entitled an "Ordinance of Caesar," it directed that graves and tombs should remain perpetually undisturbed and that capital punishment should be inflicted on anyone who demolished a tomb, displaced its seal, or maliciously transferred the dead body to another place.[10]

Most scholars agree that the ordinance was issued by the Roman emperor Claudius, who reigned from A.D. 41 to 54. At that time, grave robbing was not a capital offense in the Roman Empire. This particular decree was probably the emperor's reply to a request for guidance from a local official. We know from Roman and Jewish sources that Claudius had a scholarly mind and was a friend of Herod Agrippa I, king of Judea from A.D. 37 to 44. From Herod, Claudius had surely learned something about the Jewish religion, and perhaps even about its Christian offspring. In fact, early in his reign he had written a letter, still preserved in the British Museum, forbidding the Alexandrian Jews to bring other Jews by sea from Syria.[11] It is in the same style as the Nazareth Decree. Several years later, in A.D. 49, Claudius was sufficiently concerned about the situation that he expelled all Jews from Rome.

Putting this information together, the following scenario is a plausible explanation for the Nazareth Decree: During the first few years after Jesus' crucifixion, disputes about his tomb began to arise between Christians and Jews in Palestine. The Christians claimed it was empty because he had been raised from the dead, while the Jews claimed the Christians had stolen the body. At some

---

[10] E. M. Blaiklock, *The Archaeology of the New Testament*, pp. 75–81.
[11] Ibid., pp. 81–82.

point the disputes turned into episodes of public unrest. The matter finally came to the attention of the emperor in Rome. Claudius reigned at about the time when the unrest could be expected to have become widespread and for reports about it to have traveled back to the imperial capital. Claudius decided to put a lid on any more such controversies in his unruly province of Palestine by imposing capital punishment on anyone who desecrated a grave or removed a body. His ordinance was probably posted in various places, including Nazareth, the town where Jesus grew up and which was commonly associated with him by name, i.e., "Jesus of Nazareth," or "the Nazarene."

In this very real sense, an early Roman emperor quite possibly added his own testimony to the Christian claim that Jesus' tomb was truly empty.

The tomb was not venerated. If Jesus' tomb had not really been empty—if his decomposed corpse had still lain within it—then the site would have been venerated by his disciples and early followers as a place of special religious significance for them. In those days pious Jews often made pilgrimages to show reverence and to worship at the tombs of prominent prophets. Such ancient graves are still being visited today, e.g., the tombs of Abraham, Isaac, Jacob, and their wives in the Cave of Machpelah at Hebron, and the tomb of Rachel at Bethlehem. However, there is no record that Jesus' own tomb was similarly revered by his followers, even though by that time about fifty other Jewish tombs were being venerated.[12] The early apostolic teaching did not emphasize Jesus' tomb because, in their eyes, his bodily resurrection was of far greater importance than the tomb from which they believed he had emerged. In fact, when Peter addressed the Jerusalem crowd seven weeks after the crucifixion, he specifically contrasted the tomb

---

[12] Edwin M. Yamauchi, "Easter—Myth, Hallucination, or History?," *Christianity Today*, March 29, 1974, pp. 14–16.

containing King David's body, which he said "is here to this day," with the fact that Jesus' resurrected body "was not abandoned to the grave."[13]

The most plausible explanation for the absence of any veneration is simply that people in and around Jerusalem knew that Jesus' body wasn't in the tomb.

Admittedly, this is another argument from silence. But somewhere in the extensive writings of early Christian leaders one of them would surely have mentioned the tomb if, in fact, it had possessed any special religious significance. They commented on many other details associated with Jesus' life and death. And they wrote about the locations of the tombs for such important early Christians as Peter, John, Philip, Paul, and Polycarp.[14] Yet it was not until the fourth century, when Constantine constructed his basilica over the purported site, that the tomb of Jesus was assigned any particular religious significance.

NATURALISTIC EXPLANATIONS FOR THE EMPTY TOMB

The early Christian explanation for the empty tomb was that Jesus had been resurrected from the dead. But from the very beginning, right up to modern times, skeptics have offered alternative, non-supernatural explanations for the disappearance of his body. The theories have fallen into three categories: wrong tomb, stolen body, and live "corpse."

The women went to the wrong tomb. According to this hypothesis, the women, who were not well acquainted with Jerusalem and were walking through its narrow streets in the dim light of an early Sunday morning, mistakenly looked for Jesus' body in the wrong tomb. Not finding it there, they jumped to the

---

[13] Acts 2:29, 31.
[14] Eusebius, *The History of the Church* 2.25 (p. 63), 3.31 (p. 94), 5.24 (p. 172).

conclusion that it was missing and then hurried back through the city to tell the disciples.[15]

This explanation sounds disarmingly simple and plausible. But it contains some serious flaws.

First, if the women had gone to the wrong tomb, Jewish leaders would have been only too happy to point out the correct tomb and then produce a body. But they didn't. Not even Joseph of Arimathea made any recorded effort to deny that the tomb belonged to him and that it was empty. So the idea that the women went to the wrong tomb fails to explain a loud silence in ancient history.

Second, Jesus was buried in a private tomb, not in a public cemetery. Even in the early morning light, the women who had witnessed his crucifixion and burial would hardly have failed to recognize the particular topographical features of this single tomb and its surrounding garden, close to the place where the crucifixion had occurred.[16] Any speculation to the contrary is gossamer guesswork—admittedly possible, but not very probable.

Third, after hearing the women's story, Peter, along with John (probably the only disciple who witnessed the crucifixion[17]), ran to the tomb. They found it empty, except for the grave clothes. Their actions, in brighter morning illumination than the women had enjoyed, undercuts any notion that the women had identified the wrong tomb.

------

[15] All three synoptic Gospels state that someone at the tomb (an angel, according to Matthew and Mark, and a man, according to Luke) told the women that Jesus had risen from the dead. Matthew and Luke say that they reported this to the disciples. Mark's gospel ends abruptly (probably because the final page or two were lost at a very early date) and merely says that the women fled from the tomb in fear and said nothing to anyone. John's gospel identifies only Mary Magdalene as going to the tomb, and it makes no mention of anyone speaking to her. Mary simply told the disciples that Jesus had been taken from the tomb and put at some unknown place.

[16] John 19:41.

[17] John 19:26–27. When John referred to "the disciple whom [Jesus] loved," he was probably identifying himself.

The flimsy theory of a mis-identified tomb can hardly explain the public proclamation of the resurrection story and the rapid spread of Christianity.

Someone stole the body. From very early times the "stolen body" theory has been used to explain Jesus' empty tomb. Matthew's gospel states that the tomb guards were bribed by Jewish leaders to accuse the disciples of having stolen it,[18] and Justin Martyr states that the Jews were still repeating this story in the mid-second century.[19] Other theories have speculated that the body was stolen by Jewish authorities, by Roman authorities, or by ordinary thieves. However, a thoughtful analysis undercuts all these ideas.

With regard to the disciples, it is indeed possible to imagine that they conspired to steal Jesus' body and thereby perpetrate a monumental fraud. But it is *not* possible to imagine that this very fraud inspired them to abandon their livelihoods, devote themselves to a hard and risky missionary existence, and then end their lives as slaughtered martyrs. Such a notion is absurd on its face. All of Jesus' disciples did become missionaries, and most of them appear to have suffered the fate of martyrdom (Judas Iscariot had already committed suicide, and John probably died of old age in Asia Minor). Martyrs can be deceived, but they do not voluntarily jeopardize their lives for a hoax of their own making.

The idea that Jesus' body was stolen by his enemies, whether Jewish leaders or Roman authorities, is equally unbelievable. Within the first couple of months after the crucifixion, the Christian proclamation of Jesus' resurrection had begun its rapid spread throughout the Mediterranean world. The Jewish leaders rejected the concept that he had been their messiah and had been raised from the dead. The Roman authorities wanted to prevent religious quarrels among the Jews from escalating into civil unrest. So both the

---

[18] Matthew 28:11–15.
[19] "Dialogue with Trypho" 108, quoted by Gary R. Habermas, *Ancient Evidence for the Life of Jesus* (Nashville, TN: Thomas Nelson, 1984), p. 147.

Romans and the Jews had powerful motives for producing Jesus' corpse and putting an emphatic end to any claims about his bodily resurrection. But they did no such thing. Nowhere does Jewish literature even hint that Jesus' dead body was ever produced. Furthermore, if the Roman authorities had found it, civil unrest between Christians and Jews would never have erupted, and the most obvious explanation of Claudius's decree against grave robbing would have been eliminated. No, the idea that Jesus' body was stolen by Jews or Romans cannot be taken seriously. Neither of these groups was able to refute Jesus' alleged resurrection by parading his remains through the streets of Jerusalem.

Could ordinary thieves have stolen the body? Not likely, since they would have had no reason to break into the tomb of a man who had been crucified as a common criminal. Jesus was certainly not buried with the sort of treasure that attracts thieves. And even if they did mistakenly anticipate finding something of value, they would surely not have stolen the corpse itself.

The only other known candidate who might have played the role of thief was the wealthy Jewish leader, Joseph of Arimathea. It was his tomb. And he was certainly a real person, since any story about a nonexistent member of the Jewish ruling council would have been quickly exposed as fictitious. Perhaps, after bribing the guards and rolling away the stone seal, he removed Jesus' body and hid it at some secret location for the purpose of creating the resurrection myth. But this is highly unlikely. If Joseph was a secret Christian, as Matthew's and John's gospels state and as Mark's and Luke's gospels hint,[20] then he would have had the same motive as the disciples. He would hardly have risked his own life, or the lives of his fellow disciples, on behalf of a fraud that he himself had perpetrated. By contrast, if he was truly a pious Jew then he would have had the same motive as the Jewish leaders and would

---

[20] Matthew 27:57; John 19:38; Mark 15:43; Luke 23:50–51.

have produced the body in order to stop the Christian movement in its tracks. Either way, Joseph of Arimathea would have had no discernible reason, religious or otherwise, for removing the body and then keeping it as his own private and permanent secret.

Two final reasons undermine any claim that Jesus' body was stolen. First, John's gospel states that the grave clothes were laying in the empty tomb on Sunday morning.[21] This means that body robbers would have tarried in the tomb and taken the time to unwrap the corpse and carry it off naked—a bizarre action without any ascertainable motive. Second, Matthew's gospel relates that the tomb was secured by a large stone seal and a cadre of guards authorized by Pilate.[22] Anyone seeking to remove the body, other than someone handing out large bribes to the multitude of guards, would have had to contend with both of these formidable barriers. The stone had been set in place at the time of burial late on Friday, and the guards were posted on Saturday, probably by mid-morning. If the stone had been moved before the guards arrived, they would doubtless have noticed it. If the stone was moved after the guards were posted, it would certainly have attracted their attention (even had they been asleep), and the body snatchers would not have been able to slip silently past them.

On net balance, the "stolen body" thesis is an implausible explanation for the empty tomb.

Jesus did not die on the cross. The third naturalistic explanation for the empty tomb is that Jesus did not die on the cross. Instead, he was merely unconscious when placed in the tomb. He then regained consciousness, left the tomb, and wandered about the countryside convincing his gullible disciples that he had been resurrected from the dead.

---

[21] John 20:5–7.
[22] Matthew 27:60, 62–65. It is not entirely clear whether they were Roman guards or Jewish temple guards.

This theory, devised by a nineteenth-century German scholar,[23] asks us to accept a whole series of improbable assumptions: The Roman military executioners could not distinguish a live body on the cross from a dead one. The spear they thrust into Jesus' side was not sufficient to kill him, even if he had still been alive.[24] Inside the tomb, with lash wounds all over his body, a spear wound in his side, and spike wounds in his wrists and heels, he was single-handedly able to revive, gather strength, dislodge the stone seal, slip past the guards, and finally rejoin his disciples. He was then able to pass off his battered and bloody body as their long-awaited messiah. Common sense is nowhere to be found in these assumptions.

The business of Roman executioners was to kill condemned people, not to be duped into hauling live people down from a cross. These particular Roman soldiers were satisfied that Jesus had died on the cross. Pontius Pilate himself was also satisfied, because he permitted Joseph of Arimathea to take the corpse.[25] But even if Jesus had survived, his body would have been brutally mauled from the whipping and the crucifixion. We know from the crucified bones of Yehohanan[26] that victims were savagely nailed to their

---

[23] The theory was revived by Hugh Schonfield in *The Passover Plot* (New York: Bantam, 1967) and more recently by Holger Kersten and Elmar Gruber in *The Jesus Conspiracy* (Rockport, MA: Element Books, 1995). However, the key conclusions in these books are based on conspiratorial assumptions and tend to be (1) highly speculative reconstructions or (2) derivations from slender and ambiguous evidence, e.g., selected gospel statements, rather than the totality of the gospel accounts, and arbitrary definitions of words that in fact have obscure or multiple meanings.

[24] John 19:33–34. In his description of the spear wound, John unwittingly gave medical testimony to support the fact that Jesus was dead on the cross. A living body would have produced nothing more than spurts of red blood, but modern pathology tells us that a dead body would have oozed the two distinct fluids that John described: dark red blood clots and a separate watery serum.

[25] Matthew 27:58; Mark 15:43–45; Luke 23:52–53; John 19:38.

[26] See pp. 108–109.

crosses with large spikes through their wrists and feet. If Jesus was nailed the same way, and there is no reason to doubt that he was, then it would have been impossible for him to take even a few steps inside the tomb, much less to walk out on mangled feet and visit the various places in Jerusalem and Galilee that are described in the Gospels. So the revival theory is nothing more than unrealistic speculation.

All in all, the three naturalistic explanations for the empty tomb are short on logic and slim on evidence. By contrast, the straightforward story in the Gospels projects a far more credible ring.

Jesus' Post-Crucifixion Appearances

Standing alone, the empty tomb is circumstantial evidence. It proves nothing directly, even though the emptiness does need to be explained. Naturalistic theories have failed to provide satisfactory answers, so we are inevitably brought face to face with the possibility of a supernatural explanation: Sometime between Friday evening and Sunday morning Jesus was raised from the dead and empowered to disappear from the tomb.

This possibility cannot be dodged, although some people instinctively shy away from giving it serious consideration. Rejecting any sort of supernatural explanation as fantasy, they prefer to comfortably assume that a naturalistic explanation of the empty tomb will someday be discovered. But this attitude is akin to reasoning in a circle. It presupposes that a supernatural explanation is impossible, and then it seeks to prove this very presupposition by limiting the search to naturalistic explanations. That simply won't do. An impartial investigator does not rule out a potential answer just because he presupposes that it will not be true. Instead, he evaluates *all* potential answers before deciding which one best accounts for the known facts. If such an investigator had lived in the seventeenth century, he would not have ruled out the possibility of radio waves just because he assumed that such things could never exist.

Is there any direct evidence that Jesus was raised from the dead? Yes. It consists of eyewitness accounts that, after dying on a cross and being buried in a sealed and guarded tomb, he appeared on at least a dozen different occasions[27] to various people, at various times, in various places.[28] The people who reported these appearances believed them to be real, and the source of their belief needs to be explained by anyone who is investigating the truth of these post-crucifixion stories.

The appearances are recorded as individual episodes that seem to have occurred randomly. They are not like progressive links in a chain of illusion forged by a stage magician in the mind of his audience. Rather, they occurred at diverse times and places. Most, if not all of them, were much more than fleeting glimpses. They involved extended visits by Jesus with various people, and he spoke and acted differently on each occasion.

The appearances can be categorized in several ways. Chronologically, four of them were on the first Sunday after the crucifixion, and seven took place during the ensuing six and a half weeks, including one that occurred on the fortieth day (when Jesus is said to have ascended into heaven). The last one happened about three years later (to Paul). Geographically, six of the appearances took place in or near Jerusalem, two in Galilee, one on the road between Jerusalem and Damascus, and three in unspecified locations. They occurred in the presence of women, disciples, skeptics (James, Thomas, and Paul), and a group of more than five hundred people, many of whom would have still been available for eyewitness testimony twenty-five years later (when Paul wrote

---

[27] The appearances discussed in this chapter do not include the visions of Jesus described in Revelation, the last book of the Bible.

[28] Matthew 28:1–10, 16–20; Luke 24:13–32, 34, 36–49, 50–51; John 20:10–18, 19–25, 26–29, 21:1–23; Acts 1:4–8, 2:32, 3:15, 9:1–9, 10:41, 13:31; 1 Corinthians 15:5–8. Mark predicts the appearances (16:7) but does not describe them, probably because the last page or two of his original gospel seems to have been lost at a very early date. The last twelve verses at the end of his gospel in our English Bibles are a later addition.

about them).[29] The appearances happened both indoors and out-doors, occurring in the early morning, the midday, and the evening. With regard to attestation, some of the appearances are described by a single author—Matthew, Luke, John, or Paul—while the remaining ones are described by more than one of these authors.

As with the empty tomb, a naturalistic theory has been offered to explain the claimed appearances. It boils down to a single word: hallucinations. The appearances, it is said, were not actual visits by a risen Jesus. Rather, they were simply visions in the minds of hopeful observers.

At first glance the "hallucination" hypothesis seems rational. But, upon reflection, it presents some problems.

First, hallucinations are subjective, personal, individual experiences. They usually appear to only certain types of people, such as those with mental illness or vivid imaginations (unlike the practical and sometimes dense disciples), and they do not seem exactly the same to two different people. A single hallucination certainly does not appear to an entire group of people who come from varied backgrounds and are in different states of mind, especially when those people claim to have experienced the same details at the same time. Yet several of Jesus' alleged appearances did indeed occur to groups of people, and the Gospels even describe the various details, e.g., Jesus exhibited the nail wounds in his hands and feet, and, in a group's presence, he ate a piece of broiled fish.[30]

Second, hallucinations (except for those resulting from medical conditions) are usually the product of wishful thinking. But the disciples, and the others to whom Jesus allegedly appeared, had no prior expectation of ever seeing him again. On the contrary, after anticipating great things of Jesus while following him around Galilee and joining his triumphant entry into Jerusalem,

---

[29] 1 Corinthians 15:6.
[30] Luke 24:36–43; John 20:24–29; see also Acts 10:39–42.

their hopes were shattered when he was suddenly and ignominiously executed on a cross. The man who they believed would be a conquering Jewish messiah turned out to be just another weak victim of Roman justice. Most of the disciples scurried into hiding, utterly discouraged and dispirited. They didn't even join the women in going to the tomb for completion of the burial process on Sunday morning. These disciples had no idea that Jesus would rise from the dead and be with them again, even though he had told them several times about his coming death and resurrection.[31] In modern parlance, "they just didn't get it."

So the disciples were not engaged in hopeful anticipation when they claimed that Jesus had appeared to them. Nor was the apostle Paul, to whom the resurrected Jesus appeared on the Damascus Road. Paul was an educated Jewish rabbi, and prior to his encounter on the Damascus Road he had been an ardent persecutor of Jesus' followers. Paul was certainly engaged in no wishful thinking about a resurrection.

Not even Jewish theology, which anticipated a single resurrection for everyone at the end of time, would have nudged the subconscious minds of all these people into hoping that Jesus' dead and battered body would come back to life—much less into hallucinating that it had really happened. In fact, when Jesus appeared to the disciples in Galilee, some of them still "doubted" the reality of his resurrection.[32] This rings true as honest testimony to the authenticity—even if not the underlying meaning—of his appearances to them.

Third, hallucinations often recur over an extended period of time and may become increasingly vivid and bizarre. But the appearances of Jesus started two days after his crucifixion and (except for the appearance to Paul) ended abruptly six and a half weeks later. They did not just gradually fade away, and they exhibited no discernible trend. Throughout the entire brief period the appear-

---

[31] Mark 9:31–32; Matthew 16:21–22; Luke 9:22, 44–45.
[32] Matthew 28:16–17.

ances remained very low-key, almost prosaic, never taking on the grotesque or surreal characteristics that could be expected from a whole parade of hallucinations.

So mass hallucinations are hardly a credible explanation for the various claimed appearances of Jesus after he had died and been buried. Thus we ought to be justified in taking the gospel reports at face value. But are we?

What about the possibility that the disciples made up the stories of Jesus' appearances in order to give a factual foundation to the new faith which they set out to proclaim? If this is what happened, several questions arise. Why did the disciples admit the embarrassing fact that some of them had expressed doubts about the truth of the appearances? And if the appearances were nothing more than misrepresentations by the disciples, what can account for the apostle Paul's claimed encounter with the resurrected Jesus several years later on the Damascus Road? And don't Jesus' ongoing appearances constitute the best explanation for the disciples' seven-week delay in proclaiming their resurrection message?[33] Finally, why did the disciples fail to include a graphic description of the most important fact of all, the resurrection event itself? These are legitimate questions, which must be explained by anyone who argues that Jesus' appearances were intentional fabrications by the disciples and Paul.

Proponents of the intentional fabrication thesis must also confront the same overriding question that haunts those who hold the disciples responsible for the empty tomb: Why would men willingly embark on a life of sacrifice, and a death by martyrdom, for a fraud of their own making? Something suddenly transformed those demoralized disciples into a dynamic group of men, bound together by a mission and a message that they vigorously declared for the rest of their lives—a message that contradicted their Jewish

---

[33] Their first recorded proclamation was by Peter on Pentecost, the fiftieth day after the Passover Sabbath (the day following Jesus' crucifixion). Acts 2:1, 14–40.

heritage and that had little apparent chance of success. A self-invented hoax couldn't have done it.

Two lines of intrinsic evidence strengthen the conclusion that the gospel authors were trying to accurately report the resurrection as an historical fact.

First, the written record of the resurrection story goes too far back in Christian history to have been a legend spawned by wishful thinking. The earliest New Testament account of it appeared in A.D. 51 (some twenty years after the crucifixion), when Paul wrote his first letter to the Thessalonian church.[34] About four years later Paul reminded the members of the Corinthian church that he had preached about the resurrection when he was with them in Corinth (around A.D. 50) and that he had received his information even earlier[35] (probably by A.D. 38, when he spent two weeks with Peter in Jerusalem[36]). Luke's book of Acts, written sometime in the A.D. 60s, records the speech delivered by Peter just seven weeks after the crucifixion.[37] While addressing a large, culturally diverse crowd, Peter emphatically proclaimed the recent resurrection of Jesus as an historical fact. About thirty-five years later Peter confirmed this statement in a letter explicitly debunking the idea of a legend. He wrote that he and the others:

> did not follow cleverly invented stories. . ., but we were eyewitnesses of his [Jesus'] majesty.[38]

So directly from Paul and Peter we have evidence of a very brief period between Jesus' crucifixion and the early pronounce-

---

[34] 1 Thessalonians 1:10.

[35] 1 Corinthians 15:1–4.

[36] Galatians 1:18; Acts 9:26–29.

[37] Acts 2:14–40.

[38] 2 Peter 1:16.

ments of his resurrection. Not enough time had elapsed for germination of a legend. And even if a fictional story about a resurrection had somehow burst full-blown into fabricated gospel accounts, many living eyewitnesses could have exploded the tale right from the outset. Nobody did.

Second, the gospel accounts of the resurrection specify that women, not men, were the key players: Female followers of Jesus had been the prominent witnesses to his crucifixion and burial. They were also the ones, two days later, who discovered that his tomb was empty and reported it back to the disciples. And they were the first people to whom the purportedly resurrected Jesus made an appearance.[39]

In ancient Middle Eastern culture, like the early Christian community, if an author wanted to concoct a piece of fiction and pass it off as historically true, he would certainly not assign such a conspicuous role to women. In those days women were not treated as the equals of men. This inferior status was imposed on them right from birth. Unlike the great celebration that was triggered by the birth of a Palestinian boy, a Palestinian girl's birth was followed by a time of gloom and sorrow.[40] For the rest of her life, her testimony would be considered unreliable. So it would have made no sense for the authors of fraudulent accounts to feature people whose very gender would have damaged their credibility. On the contrary, if the authors had wanted a fictional story to be believable, they would have reported that Jesus' male followers played all the vital roles. The women would have been relegated to insignificant, peripheral functions.

But that is not the way Matthew, Mark, Luke, and John described the events. They emphasized the central role of women in critical scenes of Jesus' crucifixion, burial, and resurrection. By thus violating the cultural norm of the day, they lent powerful historical plausibility to their story of Jesus' resurrection.

---

[39] Matthew 28:8–10; John 20:14–18.
[40] William Barclay, *The Gospel of Luke*, rev. ed. (Philadelphia, PA: Westminster Press, 1975), p. 17.

We are thus left with a complex and practical question: What can explain the empty tomb, the claimed post-crucifixion appearances of Jesus, and the abrupt obliteration of Peter's cowardice, James's and Thomas's doubts, and Paul's hostility? The best answer—even though a supernatural one—seems to be the very explanation which the disciples proclaimed as historical truth: Jesus rose from the dead.

Chapter Eight

✝

THE SHROUD OF TURIN AS EVIDENCE FOR JESUS' RESURRECTION

INTRODUCTION

One other item must now be considered in connection with Jesus' claimed resurrection: the Shroud of Turin. This long, old piece of linen bears the faint image of a crucified man. If the image is a forgery, then the Shroud is irrelevant for our purpose. But if the image is genuine, then the Shroud may well constitute evidence of Jesus' resurrection.

For several reasons, this chapter is a bit risky. First, some Christians discount the Shroud because their own personal faith needs no such tangible support, especially from an artifact that is surrounded by media publicity debunking its authenticity. But this attitude is no excuse for denying skeptics the opportunity to learn about the cloth and make up their own minds about it. Second, some Christians argue that the Shroud is a fake because John's gospel states that Jesus' body was wrapped like a mummy, not enveloped in a shroud. But John's Greek words are sufficiently imprecise to allow for a single large burial shroud laid both under and over the body. Third, some Protestant Christians spurn the Shroud as "just another Catholic relic." But this cloth is utterly different from other relics. It is a uniquely identifiable artifact, subject to a rigorous scientific analysis that is not possible for generic relics (like wood claimed to have come from Jesus' cross).

For me, the Shroud of Turin is relevant to the reliability of the New Testament gospels. Therefore, it is described in this book.

DESCRIPTION OF THE SHROUD

The Shroud is probably the most controversial—and certainly the most studied—piece of cloth in the world. Many books and countless articles have been written about it.[1] Unanswered questions do remain. But perhaps this particular relic can shed light on Jesus' crucifixion, and maybe even on his alleged resurrection.

The Shroud is an old piece of linen, measuring about fourteen-and-one-half-feet long by three-and-one-half-feet wide (including a full-length seam sewn three inches from its left edge under unknown circumstances at some early date). Until a major fire in 1997, from which it was saved without damage, it had been securely housed for centuries in the cathedral of Saint John the Baptist in Turin, Italy and was seldom put on public display.

The cloth's distinguishing features are faint, front and back, full-length, yellowish sepia images of a naked man.[2] His image is slowly growing fainter because the nonimage areas of the linen are darkening with age. The man, probably Semitic, had suffered a brutal beating and a crucifixion. His body exhibits rigor mortis,

---

[1] Examples are Ian Wilson, *The Shroud of Turin*, rev. ed. (Garden City, NY: Image Books, 1979) and *The Blood and the Shroud* (New York: The Free Press, 1998); Mark Antonacci, *The Resurrection of the Shroud* (New York: M. Evans and Company, 2000); Kenneth E. Stevenson and Gary R. Habermas, *Verdict on the Shroud* (Wayne, PA: Banbury Books, 1982) and *The Shroud and the Controversy* (Nashville, TN: Thomas Nelson, 1990); Holger Kersten & Elmar R. Gruber, *The Jesus Conspiracy* (Rockport, MA: Element Books, 1995). Parts One, Two, and Four of *The Jesus Conspiracy* focus on the Shroud of Turin, while Part Three describes the authors' conclusion that Jesus did not die on the cross. For a comprehensive magazine article, see Marc Borkan, "Ecce Homo? Science and the Authenticity of the Turin Shroud," *Vertices – The Duke University Magazine of Science, Technology, and Medicine*, Vol. X, No. 2 (Winter 1995): pp. 18–51. Most of the information in this chapter is derived from these sources and has not been further footnoted.

[2] Photographs of the Shroud are contained in most books on the subject.

showing that he was dead when the image was formed.[3] He had been laid on the cloth lengthwise, probably within several hours after death, with his feet at one end and his head near the center. The remaining half of the cloth was pulled up around his head and down over his feet, serving as a cover for his entire body. When the cloth is viewed full length, the front and back images of the head are adjacent to each other in the center, and the images of the feet are at either end. The body is anatomically accurate. It shows no signs of decomposition and must therefore have been separated from the cloth within two or three days after being laid in it. When the separation occurred, the man's clearly defined bloodstains on the fabric were not even smudged.

The source of this mysterious two-part image has been the subject of controversy since the mid-fourteenth century, when the Shroud first entered recorded history as the alleged burial cloth of Jesus.

The man of the image was beaten and crucified exactly the way the Gospels describe the crucifixion of Jesus. Only two physical explanations for the image are possible: Either it was somehow produced by emanations from the man's body, or else it was a forgery designed to deceive people into thinking so. If the image is not a forgery, and if the man on the cloth was Jesus, then the Shroud of Turin certainly provides evidence for his crucifixion. Further, if modern science cannot explain the process by which the image was formed, then we need to consider the possibility that it was caused by some type of energy released from the dead body—energy that may have been connected with a resurrection of the body into a different form of existence.

---

[3] For example, the position of his legs corresponds to the position they would have had on the cross. Moreover, if he had not been dead, the blood from the wound on his side would have spurted out, not merely oozed out as revealed on the Shroud.

HISTORY OF THE SHROUD

The Shroud first appeared in the 1350s, when it was put on display by the widow of Geoffrey de Charny in the French town of Lirey, about one hundred miles southeast of Paris. To this day nobody knows how the Shroud came into possession of the Charny family. Perhaps the best hypothesis was developed by a British historian, who used numerous historical sources to reconstruct the Shroud's convoluted journey, filling in the gaps with his own estimates of likely events.[4] His reconstruction can be summarized as follows:

> Soon after the crucifixion, Jesus' burial cloth was taken to a known historical figure, King Abgar of Edessa (modern Urfa, in Turkey). When Abgar died the cloth disappeared, but around A.D. 525 it was discovered in a sealed niche within the city wall. Remaining in Edessa, it became well known to history as the *Mandylion*.[5] In A.D. 944 the cloth was taken to Constantinople (modern Istanbul). But it disappeared during the sack of the city by the Crusaders in 1204, finally reappearing in Lirey, France in the 1350s. During those 150 years, it may have been held by the secretive Knights Templar—the only group of Crusaders wealthy enough to have resisted the temptation to sell such a relic. Historical records reveal that a man named Geoffrey de Charnay, a leader in the Templars, was burned at the stake during a widespread persecution by the French king in 1314. In all likelihood, the most precious Templar treasure—Jesus' alleged burial cloth—had already been hidden away from the persecutors. It surfaced about forty years later in the family of Geoffrey de Charny, a knight of Lirey, who could well have been the great-nephew of the Templar leader.[6]

---

[4] Ian Wilson, *The Shroud of Turin*, Part IV.

[5] From a Greek word meaning "towel" and an Arabic word meaning "veil," or "handkerchief."

[6] It is also possible that the cloth, after leaving Constantinople, could have come into possession of the Charny family through ancestors of Geoffrey's wife.

The Shroud of Turin as Evidence for Jesus' Resurrection

We now switch from the British historian's blend of facts and hypothesis to facts that are well accepted. Geoffrey the knight (as distinct from Geoffrey the Templar leader) was killed in a 1356 battle against the English, and the very next year his widow decided to put the relic on public display, probably to generate needed income. A hundred years later the last member of the Charny family transferred ownership of the Shroud to the Duke of Savoy. In 1532 the folded Shroud was nearly destroyed by a fire in a Savoy chapel. The fire melted part of its silver reliquary and produced the patterns of patched and unpatched burn marks that are the Shroud's most noticeable feature today.[7] In 1578 the Savoys moved it to Turin, where it has remained ever since. Finally, when the last Savoy died in 1983, ownership passed to the Vatican.

During its centuries in Turin, the Shroud has seldom been exhibited. The first photographs of it were taken in 1898. Surprisingly, the photographic "negative" turned out to be a positive image, far more vivid and realistic than the negative image on the Shroud itself. Decades then passed before modern science was given a chance to examine the cloth. In 1973 a small sample of it was analyzed by a Belgian textile expert. Five years later, in 1978, a veritable armada of thirty-six scientists, mostly American and including six agnostics and two Jews,[8] was given five days and nights to comprehensively study the Shroud. They subjected it to batteries of exotic photographic, spectral, and other scientific analyses. Although no official report was issued, individual team members published many scientific papers in recognized, peer-reviewed journals. Nearly all members of the team discounted any notion that the image was a forgery. However, they were unable to explain how it was formed.

---

[7] Two years after the fire, in 1534, an order of nuns sewed patches onto the damaged Shroud. They also added a cloth backing to the entire Shroud in order to give it better support.

[8] John Heller, *Report on the Shroud of Turin* (Boston: Houghton Mifflin, 1983), p. 88.

Finally, in 1988, carbon-14 dating tests were performed. The three testing laboratories concluded that the linen cloth was of medieval origin, meaning it could not be the burial cloth of Jesus. Their announcement was well publicized. But the media neglected to give equal publicity to vigorous scientific criticism of the C-14 test procedures—criticism that was voiced even before the tests were conducted. And that is where matters stand in 2001.

We shall now move quickly through the primary evidence regarding the Shroud's image and try to draw a probable conclusion. However, the research details are so vast that anyone with a deeper interest should consider plunging into the voluminous literature on the subject, either from a library or over the Internet (www.shroud.com).

THE IMAGE IS NOT A FORGERY

If the Shroud of Turin is a forgery, then it is irrelevant to any review of the evidence relating to Jesus. But if it is indeed someone's burial cloth, then we must explore how a human body could have produced the image and whether that body could have been Jesus of Nazareth.

Numerous independent lines of evidence refute the notion of a forgery. They lead instead to the conclusion that the Shroud bears the actual image of a crucified man. Eight of these lines of evidence are as follows:

1. The image of the man is negative, not positive, i.e., the dark and light areas are tonally reversed from the way we see normal images. Yet a medieval forger, if he were trying to produce an image of Jesus and pass it off as genuine, would hardly have conceived of reversing all the tones. The very concept of black-and-white photography, in which a negative image is used to make a positive print, was unknown at that time. The key discovery—that silver nitrate darkens upon exposure to light—

was not definitively made until 1727, more than 350 years after the Shroud was first displayed.[9]

2. The 1978 scientific study revealed that the Shroud's image is thermally, chemically, and hydrologically stable, showing no trace of pigments, dyes, stains, or binders that might have been applied to the cloth to create the image. Nor does it show any capillarity in the threads that comprise the image. So the figure of the man could not have been painted or pressed on to the cloth. Instead, the scientists discovered that the image consists of monochromatic discoloration of the topmost fibers of the linen threads. It is similar to, but not the same as, a scorch. The scientists also found that the discoloration was produced by dehydration and oxidation. The greater the number of dehydrated fibers, the darker is the image. The discoloration does not penetrate all the way through individual threads, and thus the image does not show up on the backside of the cloth. Moreover, it does not seem to exist under the bloodstains from the man's many wounds, meaning that his blood first stained the cloth and then acted as a barrier against subsequent formation of the image itself.[10] A forger would doubtless have done it the other way around. Many attempts have been made to duplicate the process that created the Shroud's unique image. One or two have come close. But none has succeeded.[11] And

---

[9] Two British writers, in a harshly derisive book, have theorized that the image is a composite photographic negative of a dead body, produced around 1492 by Leonardo da Vinci, who utilized his own face in the process. They think he used a camera obscura (known since the time of Aristotle), a long exposure, and a rudimentary emulsion of light-sensitive salt (known to early alchemists), mixed with an organic developing material like egg white. The authors speculate that Leonardo's forgery was conspiratorially substituted for the cloth that had been exhibited in Lirey some 140 years earlier. Lynn Picknett & Clive Prince, *Turin Shroud* (New York: HarperCollins, 1994).

[10] John Heller, *Report on the Shroud of Turin*, pp. 202–3; Marc Borkan, "Ecce Homo?" p. 23.

[11] See Ian Wilson, *The Blood and the Shroud*, pp. 195–218; Mark Antonacci, *The Resurrection of the Shroud*, p. 215.

even if someone does eventually figure it out, the chances that a medieval forger would have been able to do so are virtually nil.

3. The image on the Shroud shows that the nails which fastened the man's arms to the crossbar were driven through the *wrists*. Yet all the way up through medieval times, and even to this day, artistic depictions of Jesus on the cross show the nails in his *palms*. Early artists were almost certainly ignorant of two facts: First, the Greek word *cheir*, which our English gospels translate as *hand*, can actually include the wrist. Second, the weight of a man's body on a cross could not be supported by nails driven through the palms. As modern experiments have shown, and as the Romans surely knew, a body would quickly tear away from the cross unless its weight were supported by nails driven through the bony structure of the wrist. The delicate structure of the palm simply would not do the job. A medieval forger would not have radically departed from the long artistic tradition of nails through the palms—even though it was anatomically erroneous—if he wanted his masterpiece to be accepted as genuine.

4. The hands of the man on the Shroud are crossed over his groin area, with the fingers clearly visible. But the thumbs are missing. This seems quite odd. However, according to modern medical opinion, when the spikes were driven through the man's wrists his median nerves would have been damaged or severed, thereby causing his thumbs to retract into the palms and disappear from view. Would a medieval forger have understood this physiological phenomenon? Not unless he had some experience with crucifixion—a form of punishment outlawed by the Romans in the fourth century A.D. Nor would he have painted Jesus naked in the first place. Instead, he would have followed the artistic tradition of modesty and placed a cloth around the groin.

5. The image on the Shroud shows a man whose entire scalp, including the top, had been pierced by sharp objects. Only a full *cap* of thorns would have produced this result. Yet the standard artistic tradition of Jesus on the cross shows a *wreath* of

thorns, which would have left no wounds on top of the scalp. Furthermore, the abdomen of the man on the Shroud is *swollen* (typical of asphyxiation—the normal cause of death in crucifixions), even though artistic tradition has long depicted Jesus on the cross with a *sunken* abdomen. Once again, a medieval forger would not have departed from tradition if he were trying to create a believable hoax. In fact, a medieval forger simply would not have known enough about forensic pathology to have created all the accurate anatomical details that are visible on the Shroud.

6. Several unusual substances have been found in the weave of the Shroud's linen.

First, during the 1970s a Swiss criminologist/botanist, using sticky tape sampling from twelve different areas of the cloth, discovered microscopic pollen grains from fifty-eight different species of plants. Thus, during its history, the Shroud was exposed to open air. He also found that most of the plant species grow in the vicinity of Jerusalem (some of them nowhere else) and that about half of them do not grow at all in central Europe, where a forger would probably have worked. Many of the species also grow in the regions around ancient Edessa and Constantinople, places where the Shroud has probably been. More recently, a professor emeritus at the Duke University Medical Center, using enhanced photographs of the Shroud, has discerned faint, coronal-type images of twenty-eight species of partially wilted Palestinian flowers and plants.[12] Appearing individually and in bunches, each of the plants grows in or near Jerusalem. All but one of them bloom in March and April, the very time of year in which Jesus was likely crucified. Of the twenty-eight species, twenty-five of them match, or are closely related to, the pollen grains found on the Shroud. These

---

[12] Alan D. and Mary W. Whanger, "Evidence of Early Origin and Nature of the Shroud of Turin by Image Analysis and Optical Comparison," paper presented at the International Symposium on the Shroud of Turin, Columbia University, New York City (March 2, 1991).

findings of pollen grains and plant images have been confirmed by two respected Israeli botanists.

Second, the Belgian textile expert who examined a cloth sample from the Shroud in 1973 ascertained that the loom on which the linen was woven had also been used to weave cotton. The cotton fibers were of a type long grown in the Middle East, but nowhere else.

Third, in 1978 microscopic dirt particles were discovered deep in the cloth. They appeared only around the heel images (showing that the man had walked barefoot to the cross) and the knee and nose images (where they were mixed with blood from abrasions, indicating that he had fallen).[13] In addition, the Shroud contains traces of calcium that match the uncommon type of limestone found in the rock shelf where Jesus was buried in Jerusalem. None of the limestone from nine other burial sites in Israel produced such a match.[14]

Putting all these findings together, it is unreasonable to assume that a medieval forger would have found a linen cloth containing pollen grains from Palestine, cotton fibers from the Middle East, dirt particles right at the foot, knee, and nose images, and microscopic residue of Jerusalem limestone. It is equally unreasonable to assume that he figured out which species of flower was produced by each of the invisible pollen grains and then decided to add images of those particular floral species to his forgery.

7. The image of the man contains one surprising characteristic, which was hidden until the 1970s. At that time an old photograph of the Shroud was tested with NASA's VP-8 image analyzer, a device using radar-type data to determine surface contours by means of image intensities. It interprets darker parts of an image as being farther away. When applied to a two-dimensional photo of the Shroud, the VP-8 unexpectedly reproduced an accurate, three-dimensional relief of the man. In other

---

[13] John Heller, *Report on the Shroud of Turin*, pp. 112, 152.
[14] Mark Antonacci, *The Resurrection of the Shroud*, p. 109.

words, the 2-D Shroud image contains encoded 3-D information—something never found in ordinary photographs or paintings of human beings. A forger would have had no way to do this.

8. Art history provides our final line of evidence supporting the image's authenticity. In the first few centuries after Jesus' death, his physical appearance was artistically depicted in many different ways. But in the sixth century this suddenly changed. Certain specific details about Jesus' face, similar to those in the face of the man on the Shroud (e.g., hairline, eyebrows, mustache, lips, and beard) started to be included in most artistic paintings and murals. They even appeared on Byzantine coins. For example, two small, nonidentical gold coins bearing the face of Jesus, minted by Justinian II in the seventh century A.D., exhibit many detailed characteristics that are identical to the face on the Shroud. Could all these artistic similarities have abruptly appeared by coincidence? Possibly, but not probably. The most logical explanation is that when the Shroud (soon to be known as the *Mandylion*) was discovered in the city wall of Edessa around A.D. 525, it was quickly adopted by artists as their standard depiction of Jesus.

So eight independent lines of evidence strongly support the image's authenticity. When combined with each other, and with various additional items of evidence appearing on the cloth, they refute the theory of a medieval forgery.

Against this evidence, what do opponents of authenticity point to? Up until 1988 they typically relied on an unsigned and undated copy of a memorandum, probably written by a French bishop around A.D. 1389, which described how one of his predecessors had found the Shroud to be a painting. They also argued that the reconstructed history of the Shroud is highly speculative and doesn't really explain where the cloth came from or where it has been. Finally, they sometimes argued that the blood flows on the body do not entirely comport with physiological reality (admittedly, the blood flows exhibit some uncertainty). But their most powerful argument suddenly emerged in 1988. On October 13, three laboratories announced that carbon-14 dating tests had proved, with 95 percent probability, that the Shroud's linen came from flax that had been grown in the thirteenth or fourteenth century. Therefore it clearly could not have been Jesus' burial cloth. But do the C-14 tests definitively debunk the Shroud? Not really.

THE CARBON-14 TEST DID NOT EXPOSE A FRAUD

Carbon is constantly being absorbed by all living organisms. A tiny portion of it is in the form of a radioactive isotope called carbon-14. When an organism dies it stops absorbing new carbon. At the same time, its existing supply of radioactive C-14 begins to steadily decay. By measuring the amount of the organism's remaining C-14, as a portion of its total carbon content, the approximate date of the organism's death can be estimated.

The C-14 tests on the Shroud were conducted by laboratories in Zurich, Oxford, and Tucson. A single, small piece was removed from the cloth and then divided into smaller pieces. Under supervision by the British Museum, one of the smaller pieces was given to each lab. After testing, the three labs concluded that the linen was made of flax which had been grown between A.D. 1260 and 1390. If they were right, then the Shroud is a medieval forgery.

But is it? Not likely. As scientists often point out, C-14 testing is not the sole answer for dating old objects. It provides only one line of evidence. In the case of the Shroud, C-14 test results must be weighed against the many lines of other evidence that support a much older age. Refusal to consider this other evidence violates normal scientific method. It also ignores the fundamental principle that each side in a debate must undertake two distinct tasks: first, the presentation of its own affirmative case and, second, the response to arguments offered by the other side. So people who offer the C-14 test as conclusive proof that the Shroud is a fake cannot just walk away from the compelling evidence for its authenticity, any more than proponents of authenticity can walk away from the C-14 test results.

Moreover, for at least a half dozen reasons the particular C-14 test conducted on the Shroud falls short of providing solid support for the forgery theory.

1. Contrary to the recommendations in a formal 1986 scientific protocol, the testing was limited to three laboratories. Each one used accelerator mass spectrometry, a new technique that measured individual atoms but which had seldom been used to date pieces of cloth. Excluded from the testing were two laboratories using the proportional counter technique, a process that measured radioactivity and which had long been the conventional method for dating cloth. Ironically, even the three laboratories that had been chosen expressed dismay that other labs had not been allowed to participate.[15] And the 1978 STURP study team was also shut out of the testing, even though some of its members were prepared to assist in selection of the cloth samples and to arrange for a wide array of follow-up chemical and physical tests on the Shroud.

2. During test runs, the three selected labs came up with widely conflicting and incorrect dates for pieces of cloth from control samples. One such sample was an Egyptian burial cloth with a known age from 3000 B.C. Each laboratory tested it and then assigned a date. All three dates were too recent, and the oldest and youngest ones were about eleven hundred years apart. Even the estimated age from the lab that came the closest was nearly five hundred years too young. These sorts of radically inaccurate and divergent results, which were attributed to contamination of the cloth, do not inspire much confidence in the C-14 testing that the three labs later conducted on the Shroud of Turin. Confidence is further eroded by a drawing in a Budapest prayer manuscript, dated from A.D. 1192. The upper panel shows Jesus' naked body, positioned like the man on the Shroud, with

---

[15] Joseph Marino, "The Shroud of Turin and the Carbon 14 Controversy," *Fidelity* (February 1989): p. 38.

four fingers on each hand and without any thumbs. This is strong evidence that the twelfth-century artist was familiar with the thumbless image on the Shroud. Equally strong evidence of the Shroud's pre-thirteenth century date is revealed on the lower panel of the Budapest manuscript. It depicts Jesus' burial cloth, with the distinctive herringbone weave of the Shroud. Clearly visible on the panel is a pattern of four small holes, precisely congruent with four small burn holes that are prominent on the Shroud today. They had to have been burned into the cloth before the Budapest drawing was created in A.D. 1192. Yet, according to the C-14 test, this would have been up to two hundred years *before* the Shroud even existed—a chronological impossibility.[16]

3. C-14 testing is most accurate on artifacts that have remained undisturbed throughout their history. But this certainly doesn't describe the Shroud, which was moved, handled, and displayed many times over the centuries. During that long period of time, it was often exposed to contaminants like oil, wax, starch, mold, soap, sweat, and smoke, all of which added to its carbon content. This problem was recognized as far back as the 1960s, when scientists warned that ancient contamination would distort any C-14 testing of the Shroud.[17]

Another form of contamination was identified in 1993 by a microbiology specialist at the University of Texas. While examining some pieces of the Shroud that had been trimmed off from the C-14 testing samples five years earlier, he discovered that the linen fibers were coated with a clear bioplastic material. It was comprised of natural bacteria and fungi that had steadily accumulated over the centuries, much like the buildup

---

[16] Holger Kersten & Elmar Gruber, *The Jesus Conspiracy*, pp. 173–174; Ian Wilson, *The Blood and the Shroud*, pp. 145–147.
[17] Ian Wilson, *The Blood and the Shroud*, pp. 190–191.

of plaque on teeth.[18] The coating contains carbon-14, some of it from the bacteria and fungi that are still alive and absorbing more carbon. It should be noted, however, that several scientists have expressed doubts that the bioplastic material could have added enough C-14 to significantly alter the Shroud's carbon dating test results.

4. Prior to the C-14 testing, scientists had recommended that seven test samples be taken, each from a *separate* and *undamaged* section of the Shroud. But this recommendation was ignored. Only one sample was taken. Unfortunately, it came from the lower left corner of the cloth, an area where extensive human handling had occurred over the centuries and which had been heavily contaminated during the 1532 fire. It was also adjacent to the sidestrip seam of unknown history and contamination. In fact, a video of the cutting procedure seems to show that threads from the seam were actually included in the test sample. So the three laboratories, each of which received one part of the sample, were merely conducting three repetitions of a single test on a single polluted sample.

5. If Jesus was truly the man on the Shroud, and if in fact he was resurrected from the dead, then his image was likely imprinted by some sort of sudden burst of radiation from his body. This process could have included the release of neutrons. Such a release can alter the nuclei of carbon-13 and nitrogen-14 atoms (both of which are present in the Shroud), converting them into carbon-14 atoms. If the Shroud is indeed from the first century A.D., an increase of only 18% in its C-14 content would

---

[18] Ten years earlier the specialist had discovered such a coating on an allegedly ancient Mayan artifact. The carving had been thought to be a recent fake because of its shiny appearance. The scientist analyzed the coating and concluded that it was a naturally occurring phenomenon and did not indicate a recent origin. During the ensuing years he identified similar coatings on many ancient Mayan artifacts. Ian Wilson, *The Blood and the Shroud*, pp. 223–231.

have shifted its true date (about A.D. 30) to a "tested" date of around A.D. 1350—right into the range calculated by the labs at Zurich, Oxford, and Tucson. To illustrate, in recent experiments two mummy samples were carbon dated to the second century B.C. They were then irradiated with neutrons and subjected to fire simulation (like the 1532 Shroud fire). Thereafter, following the kind of pretreatment cleaning used by the three labs on the Shroud sample, a second carbon dating was performed. It showed these same samples to be from the Middle Ages—an age shift of thirteen or fourteen centuries younger than the first test had shown.[19]

6. In the early 1990s, two German researchers developed a conspiracy theory.[20] Conspiracies are easy to allege, but this one is not entirely implausible. The researchers describe well-documented clashes and maneuvers among scientific and ecclesiastical egos before the C-14 test procedures had been finalized. They highlight the sloppy controls that surrounded the testing process itself, preventing it from being a truly blind evaluation. They also argue that the Catholic Church, fearful that the Shroud provided evidence for Jesus' survival on the cross, wanted it to fail the C-14 test. This was allegedly accomplished by privately substituting samples from a medieval cloth in place of the samples that had been publicly cut from the Shroud.

The overall conclusion to be drawn from the C-14 test is quite simple: Even putting aside the conspiracy theory, the sampling was careless, the procedures were amateurish, and the participants were unconcerned about the various lines of evidence supporting an early date for the Shroud. All in all, it does not appear to have been a sterling scientific procedure. So C-14, standing alone, should not be glibly offered as conclusive proof that the image is a medieval forgery.

---

[19] Mark Antonacci, *The Resurrection of the Shroud*, pp. 159–164.
[20] Holger Kersten & Elmar Gruber, *The Jesus Conspiracy*.

The Shroud of Turin as Evidence for Jesus' Resurrection

WAS JESUS THE MAN ON THE SHROUD?

The evidence points to the Shroud as a genuine first-century Jewish burial cloth. But was Jesus of Nazareth the man whom it once enclosed? Absolute proof does not exist. Yet every specific gospel detail about Jesus' crucifixion is exhibited on the cloth.

1. The area under the man's right eye is severely swollen. The Gospels report that, before crucifying Jesus, Pilate's soldiers repeatedly struck him on the head with a staff.[21]
2. The man's back and legs reveal many dumbbell-shaped whip marks, corresponding precisely with a known form of Roman whip called a *flagrum*. According to the Gospels, Jesus was flogged before being crucified.[22]
3. Numerous small blood streams are prominent on the man's forehead and on the top and back of his head.[23] The Gospels describe how Roman soldiers twisted together a crown of thorns, which they set upon Jesus' head.[24]
4. The man's back shows distinct abrasions on his shoulders from an object rubbing against them after the flogging had been

---

[21] Matthew 27:30; Mark 15:19.

[22] Matthew 27:26; Mark 15:15; John 19:1.

[23] Additional blood streams appear from the wrist wounds, at the very angles they would have flowed "up" the arms of a crucified victim whose shoulders were sagging below the level of his nailed wrists. Nevertheless, the blood flows do pose a problem. If the body was placed in the Shroud without being washed, the wounds should have bled much more profusely than revealed by the cloth. But if the body was placed in the Shroud after having been washed, the blood flow angles on the cloth from the thorn and nail wounds would be inconsistent with a body lying on a slab. The various "bloodstains" on the Shroud were tested by members of the 1978 study team. They are real human blood of a person who had suffered severe trauma. John Heller, *Report on the Shroud of Turin,* pp. 142–7, 186; Mark Antonacci, *The Resurrection of the Shroud,* pp. 25–29.

[24] Matthew 27:28–29; Mark 15:17.

finished. John's gospel mentions that Jesus went to the place of crucifixion "carrying his own cross."[25]

5. The man's side was pierced by a large, pointed instrument, like a Roman lance. Both blood and serum oozed from this postmortem wound and on to the Shroud. John's gospel emphasizes that just such a wound was inflicted on Jesus, evidently to confirm that he had already died, and that "blood and water" flowed from the wound.[26]

6. The legs of the man on the Shroud were not broken, even though the Romans customarily did so as a means of hastening death. John's gospel points out that the legs of the two men crucified along with Jesus were broken. But John also states that the soldiers did not break the legs of Jesus, because he was already dead.[27]

HOW WAS THE IMAGE FORMED?

As noted earlier, the image on the Shroud was not produced by pigment, dye, or stain. So it wasn't a painting or pressing process. Nor could it have been a vapor emanating from the body, which would have produced a diffuse image, not the clear and delicate one exhibited on the Shroud. And a direct contact process could not have produced the Shroud's noticeable shadings or the 3-D effect that is encoded in the cloth. Finally, scientific fluorescence tests have ruled out any known form of heat scorch. So none of these processes can account for the image.

One additional problem in explaining the image is the mystery of how something that looks like a *flat* photograph could have been transferred on to a cloth that was draped in a *curve* over a human body. If the body itself produced the image on the Shroud, we would expect that the sides of the man's arms, hips, and legs would have been at least partially visible on the cloth. This would

---

[25] John 19:17.
[26] John 19:34.
[27] John 19:33.

make the body appear unnaturally wide when the linen is stretched flat. But that is not what we see. Instead, when the Shroud is stretched flat the image is undistorted, showing a perfectly proportioned man just as though he had been photographed through a camera lens on to a flat piece of film. If the Shroud once served as that flat piece of film, then, in theory, an accurate image could have been focused and projected on to it. But this is not a realistic possibility. Back in Jesus' time, the concept of photographic films and developing chemicals lay eighteen hundred years in the future. Nevertheless, the front and back images on the Shroud are exactly what would be expected if every pore and hair on the man's body had contained a tiny laser and all the beams had been projected vertically up onto the curved cloth above him and down onto the flat cloth beneath him.

So where does that leave us in trying to explain the image on the Shroud? What kind of process could have created it? Suffice to say, the scientists currently have no firm explanation. Their experiments with secondary X-radiation and coronal discharge seem to have come closest to producing Shroud-like images on dry cloth.[28] But no such processes would have been available to a human forger seven hundred years ago.

The search for a cause of the Shroud's image will doubtless continue, and every hypothesis will need to be tested by its success in explaining all the observed characteristics of the image. Future testing will be vital. For example, neutron irradiation should be explored in order to evaluate whether radiation caused both the image and the anomalous 1988 C-14 results. The necessary samples could be obtained from uncharred portions of the original

---

[28] Radioactive illumination has produced on cellulose fibers the same sort of straw-yellow image found on the Shroud. Mark Antonacci, *The Resurrection of the Shroud*, p. 223. In coronal discharge, a high-energy electrical field is created, spreading its energy over the surface of all irregularly shaped or pointed objects in the field. When the current is discharged, an ionization process leaves images of the objects on their cloth covering. Kenneth E. Stevenson and Gary R. Habermas, *The Shroud and the Controversy*, pp. 41–2.

fabric lying under the patches from the 1532 fire. One such test could determine whether the Shroud contains any calcium-41, which would have been produced by neutron irradiation of the calcium-40 that is distributed throughout the Shroud. Another test, requiring small samples of the Shroud's bloodstains, could determine the presence of chromium-53, which would have been produced by neutron irradiation of iron in the man's blood.[29] Yet even if a reproducible cause of the image is someday discovered, two nagging questions will linger: Could this cause have occurred as a natural phenomenon? And why did this kind of image appear only once among all the thousands of funerary cloths that have come down to us from human history?

The most probable answer to the two questions might just be this: No known phenomenon could have produced the image. Instead, it was created when God intervened and resurrected Jesus from the dead. During that process some form of radiant energy was released, leaving behind his undistorted image on the burial cloth, perhaps imprinted as the linen collapsed through the void left by the dematerializing corpse.[30] Then, in a resurrected body, Jesus emerged from the tomb, leaving behind the cloth that bore his image and his undisturbed bloodstains.

This may sound fanciful. But nobody witnessed the resurrection. So some such sequence of events must be offered as an explanation of how the image came into existence. The simple fact may well be that the Shroud of Turin is a tangible piece of evidence for Jesus' resurrection. If so, it would also be evidence for his divinity and for the very existence of God.

CONCLUSION

The resurrection of Jesus forms the centerpiece of Christianity. If it actually occurred, then the other pieces fall readily into place. But absolute proof of the resurrection will continue to elude us,

---

[29] Mark Antonacci, *The Resurrection of the Shroud*, pp. 185–191.
[30] Ibid., pp. 222–232.

just as it does with all ancient historical events. Instead, we must be satisfied with some level of probability. The entire thrust of chapter seven and this chapter has been to place the resurrection claim within the context of the historically credible gospel records and then to examine the particular evidence that relates to the resurrection itself. It stands up well. The tomb was surely empty. The alleged post-crucifixion appearances are hard to explain as fantasies. And the Shroud of Turin just might be a forensic fingerprint of the event itself.

All in all, the case for the resurrection is strong. A person can choose to deny it. But the weight of the evidence supports a conclusion that God did indeed resurrect Jesus and that he thereby validated all of Jesus' claims about himself.

Chapter Nine

✝

THE COMMON SENSE OF CHRISTIANITY

INTRODUCTION

The New Testament gospels are a credible and corroborated record of Jesus' birth, life, death, and resurrection. But credibility and corroboration cannot create an absolute *certainty* that all the events described in the Gospels actually happened or that all the spoken words were precisely transcribed. The best they can do is make the record *probable*, thereby leading to a high level of confidence that the Gospels are historically true. Yet intellectual confidence, standing alone, is not enough. Christianity requires some degree of faith. It may be a short step, or it may be a long leap. But it is faith nonetheless. It is "being *sure* of what we hope for and *certain* of what we do not see."[1]

This chapter and chapter ten are written for people who have assigned a reasonably high probability to the historical veracity of the Gospels, but who are struggling with the required layer of faith. Some of these people balk because they have specific criticisms of Christian theology, churches, and people. Obstacles of that sort will be addressed in chapter ten. But for other people the problem is more general: Christianity doesn't satisfy their instinctive feelings of common sense. It just doesn't quite hang together. For such people, this chapter assesses the inherent plausibility of Christianity, with the objective of demonstrating that a sensible skeptic need not abandon his or her good judgment in order to take a step of

---

[1] Hebrews 11:1 (emphasis added).

Christian faith. No additional evidence will be presented. No degree of faith will be assumed. Rather, in order to eliminate a potential obstacle to a step of faith, we will simply examine whether Christian belief is *inherently* consistent and sensible.

The Reality of Human Misbehavior

Every society adopts fundamental standards for proper behavior. Some are manmade and subject to continual modification, like our complex web of criminal and civil legal requirements. Others derive from firmly fixed religious precepts, like the Ten Commandments.[2] All of the standards prescribe conduct that is accepted by most people. But everybody occasionally violates some of them. When that happens, the standard serves as a spotlight, illuminating the misconduct through the person's conscience.[3]

These manmade and religious standards show that individual people cannot always trust each other to do what is "right." Everyone exhibits a universal human tendency toward misbehavior.[4] Not a single one of us unfailingly measures up to either the manmade standards or the religious standards.[5] In fact, few of us consistently measure up to even our own personal standards. Virtually everyone—even those who believe that "I'll get to heaven because I'm a good person"—instinctively agrees that we do not always act "properly." This truth was elegantly expressed nearly 500 years ago by the Swiss reformer, Ulrich Zwingli:

---

[2] Exodus 20:1–17; Deuteronomy 5:6–21.

[3] Romans 3:20.

[4] "Misbehavior" is not always easy to define. For example, within the context of governmental laws and activities, a peaceful sit-in to protest racially discriminatory statutes is seldom called misbehavior, although technically it may violate the law or someone's property rights. But the bombing of a government building as a form of protest goes far beyond acceptable limits. For purposes of this chapter we shall assume a definition of legal misbehavior on which most people would agree, whether it is a traffic violation or attempted murder.

[5] Romans 3:23.

Who, pray, can shine with such purity as to walk without blemish. . .? Or who among mortals is so single-hearted that neither his heart nor his tongue has ever practiced deceit?. . .In whose eyes have the evil always been despised and the good held in high esteem. . .when. . .we are all hypocrites and have all sinned and fallen short of the glory of God?[6]

In Judeo-Christian terminology, such misbehavior is described by the intimidating little word, *sin.* This powerful, tiny word covers not just massive misbehavior like murder, but *all* forms of misbehavior, both major and minor.

So how does God view the situation?

THE BIBLE'S STATEMENT OF GOD'S ATTITUDE TOWARD HUMAN SIN

The Old and New Testaments teach that God is holy. His moral standards are both high and strict. According to the Old Testament, no one is holy like God.[7] He is too pure to look upon evil, and he cannot tolerate wrong.[8] King David underscored this reality by writing that no one can dwell with God *except* a person:

whose walk is blameless and who does what is righteous. . .who does his neighbor no wrong and. . .who keeps his oath even when it hurts. . .[9]

In other words, sin offends God's holy character. As a result, he cannot allow sinful people to enter into his eternal presence. And therein lies our problem, because every one of us has committed wrongs of one sort or another. From God's viewpoint, all these

---

[6] *Commentary on True and False Religion* (Durham, NC: Labyrinth Press, 1981), pp. 101–102.
[7] 1 Samuel 2:2.
[8] Habakkuk 1:13.
[9] Psalm 15.

wrongful acts are sins.[10] As the perpetrators, we must each accept eternal responsibility for the ones that we commit. We cannot assume that making excuses and whining to God will get us off the hook. The God of the Bible is certainly not presented as some gullible grandfather who pats his misbehaving grandchildren on the head, gives them a wink, and offers a tolerant platitude like, "Don't worry, I won't tattle to Mom or Dad." God's very essence prevents him from allowing us to escape so easily. He cannot routinely ignore our misbehavior.

At this point, many people take refuge in the warm and fuzzy notion that if a person's good deeds outweigh his or her bad deeds, then a loving God will tolerate the minor transgressions—and maybe even a few of the major ones. However, according to the Bible, this is not the way it works. God's attributes are not limited to love. They also include righteousness, meaning that he abhors even a single bad deed.[11] It's easy to focus exclusively on God's attribute of love and to ignore his insistence upon justice and righteousness. It's comforting to assume that God will put each person's life on a balance scale, and will allow entrance into eternal life with him—heaven—if the good deeds outweigh the bad ones. But this happy vision could well be a dangerous delusion. In fact, within the context of Christian belief, it doesn't make a whole lot of sense. God refuses to be contaminated by just a single sinful act, even if it is committed by the world's nicest person.

If eternal life with God depended on a positive balance of good deeds in a person's lifetime ledger, nobody would ever know whether his or her ledger had enough good entries to qualify. Unanswerable questions would abound: Who defines whether a deed is "good" or "bad"? Will it take a 90–10 ratio of good deeds to bad ones, or will a 51–49 ratio be enough? How important is motive? Will all deeds be weighted equally? The list is endless. Thus, as a

---

[10] Jesus pointed out that sinful conduct emanates from within people's hearts, making all of us "unclean." Mark 7:21–23.

[11] "'Cursed is everyone who does not continue to do *everything* written in the Book of the Law.'" Galatians 3:10 (emphasis added); Daniel 9:14.

practical matter, the balance scale analysis prevents anyone from ever knowing whether the gates of heaven will be open for him or her. It bogs people down in a nightmare of uncertainty.

The pleasant analogy of a balance scale may be an interesting exercise. But it is nothing more than that. Conceptually and practically, it is flawed. And as a way of figuring out who gets to spend eternity with God, it is useless.

Thus we seem to face an inexorable conclusion: Unless God relaxes his standards, nobody will ever be allowed into his eternal presence. After death, each of us will spend eternity apart from God or, at best, simply disappear into nothingness.

This dismal result surely runs contrary to God's attribute of love. But if he does indeed want people to enter heaven, what can he do to make it happen? He cannot relax his standards, because his own holiness prevents him from having eternal fellowship with people whose lives have been polluted by sinful behavior. This includes all of us. So *nobody* would make it into heaven, and we are right back where we started. God needed to design a plan that would satisfy his attribute of love by somehow overlooking a person's sins and judging him or her in such a way that the sins would be totally forgiven and treated as if they had never actually happened. But the plan would also need to satisfy God's righteousness, i.e., it would have to require some sort of penalty for a person's sinful behavior. He or she could not be allowed to escape accountability.

Christians define God's solution for achieving these twin objectives—love and righteousness—as "grace." The apostle Paul succinctly described it as follows:

> [I]t is by grace you have been saved, through faith—and this not from yourselves, it is the gift of God—not by works [deeds], so that no one can boast.[12]

---

[12] Ephesians 2:8–9.

GOD'S MECHANISM OF GRACE

According to the New Testament, God's mechanism of grace is a simple plan that avoids the conceptual and practical problems of the balance scale approach: He came to Earth as a real person, paid for all human misbehavior by allowing himself to be killed, and thereby offered a passport of grace to everyone who accepts him as who he claimed to be. The New Testament teaches that people who take hold of the passport during their lifetimes will be assured of two things: first, a relationship with God during the remainder of their lives on Earth and, second, eternal lives with God after their human time on Earth is finished. Those who reject the passport will, according to Christian belief, face present and eternal separation from God.[13] And even if the Christian belief were false, they would face an uncertain eternity.

God's plan for bringing human beings into heaven recognizes that everyone has committed acts which are contrary to God's desire and that a penalty must be paid to satisfy his attribute of righteousness. God himself paid the penalty on their behalf. If they accept the payment, then God will implement his grace and overlook all their underlying misbehavior. However, if they reject it, then their lives will not be acceptable to God. They will not stand in true friendship with him on Earth and will not be able to spend eternity with him after death.

Perhaps God could have selected some other way to deal with the sins of humankind. Maybe he could have intimidated everyone into a relationship with him by some sort of brilliant celestial display and a booming voice from the sky. But a glitzy extravaganza would not have produced an authentic faith and a genuine love for God. So coming to Earth as a human being was the way God chose to do it. Some of us may not like his plan. But it was God's choice, not ours. And, upon reflection, it makes good sense. People can decide for themselves whether to accept his passport of grace. If they do, then they are freed from the guilt of past misbe-

---

[13] John 3:18.

havior. They are also freed from the burden of uncertainty about a right relationship with him and about entry into heaven. But if they reject the passport, then they will have to accept the consequences of their own misbehavior. There will be no loopholes.

Jesus Serves as God's Mechanism of Grace

According to the Christian faith, and based upon the Gospels, a single God exists in the persons of the Father, the Son, and the Holy Spirit. The inner workings of this triune concept are beyond our ability to fully understand. But the Gospels do state that the Son came to Earth in human form as Jesus of Nazareth. His humanity is vividly portrayed: He was born full term to a woman. He had normal human needs, such as food and water. He had normal human emotions, such as sorrow and anger. He was tempted by sin, but, unlike the rest of us, he always resisted it. He physically died and was buried. And, as a demonstration of his divinity, he was resurrected from the dead. In other words, the New Testament teaches that Jesus was both fully divine and fully human.

As a human being, Jesus lived a sinless life and then voluntarily offered it as a substitute payment for all the sins of mankind. He himself became God's passport of grace, issued to people who truly embrace a genuine faith in his identity, death, and resurrection.[14] These people will thereafter be viewed by God through the lens of Jesus' sinlessness. Their previous good deeds will not *cause* them to become eligible for the passport, but thereafter their good deeds—and their reduced number of bad deeds—will be the normal *result* of having received it. Paul described the passport quite succinctly:

> [I]f you confess with your mouth, "Jesus is Lord," and believe in your heart that God raised him from the dead, *you will be saved.*[15]

---

[14] John 3:16, 36.
[15] Romans 10:9 (emphasis added).

On a practical level, God's decision to offer Jesus as the solution to humanity's dilemma made good sense. It opened the way for God to speak directly to men and women in a human voice, in their own language, on their own level, in their own environment, and as one who shared their own emotions. God did not choose to overpower people with a thunderous proclamation of his message. Nor did he choose to speak to each person's conscience so subtly that few would really listen. Instead, his technique of becoming human allowed people to *understand* his message without *forcing* them into any particular response one way or the other.

God's decision also made conceptual sense, because Jesus, as a human being, was subject to all the temptations that are encountered by people everywhere. The fact that he did not succumb to the temptations allows him to be a role model for all of us. By contrast, if God had sent Jesus to Earth in the form of nothing more than a visible spirit, people could legitimately refuse to look upon him as a teacher and a role model. They could dodge the issue of their own misbehavior by rationalizing that it was easy for Jesus to proclaim lofty standards of human conduct, since he himself was not human and was not enticed by the human sins that he condemned. But this excuse is not available to us, because Jesus delivered his message as a human being who was subject to exactly the same temptations as his audience. His human ability to resist these temptations brings his message much closer to our own lives than if he had arrived as a spiritual apparition.

After preaching for about three years, Jesus was crucified. As a real human being, he voluntarily allowed himself to be put to a brutal death. By doing so, he provided a powerful example to comfort and strengthen other people who also must endure suffering.

More importantly, however, is this: When Jesus was near death, God temporarily turned his back on this man who had lived a sinless life. In response, Jesus uttered a very human cry, "My God, my God, why have you forsaken me?"[16] This cry revealed that Jesus, as a real person, was voluntarily suffering a spiritual death—

[16] Matthew 27:46; Mark 15:34.

separation from God the Father. Thus God's attribute of righteousness and justice was being satisfied. Jesus was the *one* person in human history who did *not* deserve to be forsaken by God. In a very real sense, this man, who owed nothing, was voluntarily paying to God the debt that had been, and would continue to be, accumulated by the misbehavior of the entire human race. As Jesus himself said, he came to Earth in order "to give his life as a ransom for many."[17] Individual people cannot pay their own debt. Much less can they do it for each other. It could only have been paid by someone—Jesus of Nazareth—who had incurred no debt in the first place.[18]

To summarize the concept of what happened at the cross, it might be useful to think of a traffic judge whose teenage child stands before him in court. The child is guilty, but has no money to pay a penalty. So, after determining the amount of the fine, the judge steps down from the bench, takes on the role of a father, and makes payment to the clerk out of his own pocket. This satisfies the judge's duty to impose justice. But it also displays the love of a father who voluntarily pays a debt he does not owe.

Two Questions About Heaven

In the New Testament Paul explains that Jesus laid the foundation, i.e., became the passport, for entering heaven. But Paul went on to explain that once a person arrives in heaven his rewards will be proportionate to the *quality of his works* on Earth.[19] We can only speculate about the nature of these rewards, just as we can only speculate about the nature of heaven itself. The most that can be said with assurance is that eternity *with* a God who wants to have a loving relationship with us forever will doubtless be better than eternity *without* him. And, by definition, it will be better than

---

[17] Mark 10:45.

[18] 2 Corinthians 5:21.

[19] 1 Corinthians 3:11–15; Ephesians 6:8.

no eternity at all. But two difficult and closely related questions are sometimes asked.

First, is it fair for someone who accepts God's passport of grace late in life (or who accepted it early and then died young), and who thus had little time to perform many high-quality works, to get into heaven just as easily as someone who had accepted the passport at a young age and then had spent a full lifetime performing such works? This reasonable question received a response from Jesus himself. In one of his parables he described heaven in terms of a man who owned a vineyard. Early one morning he hired some workers, agreeing to pay them a certain amount of money for the day. Then at various times throughout the day he hired other workers, specifying no particular amount. At the end of the day, he paid each worker exactly the same amount. Predictably, the workers who had been hired early in the morning grumbled about the unfairness of not receiving more than those who worked only an hour or two. The owner's response was simple:

> I am not being unfair to you. Didn't you agree to work for a denarius?[20] . . .Don't I have the right to do what I want with my own money? Or are you envious because I am generous?[21]

The same lesson applies to us. God has the right to be generous to everyone who accepts his passport of grace, even to people who do so very late in their lives or who accept it early and then die young.

This leads to the second issue. Even though God has the right to be generous to people who had little *time* to perform good works on Earth, Paul writes that the rewards for Christians in heaven will nevertheless vary from person to person according to the *quality* of their works on Earth. Such a result seems equitable. Those who perform better deeds on Earth will receive proportionately greater rewards in heaven. But if this is true, what about the potential for

---

[20] A typical day's pay. It was the equivalent of what a Roman soldier received.
[21] Matthew 20:1–15.

envy and strife in heaven? Wouldn't the contaminating presence of jealousy and conflict violate our belief that heaven will be a serene and pleasant place? The question has no clear-cut answer.

One way to look at the subject is by using the illustration of a sporting event. Suppose two people each receive a free ticket to an upcoming baseball game. They both know the basic rules of the game, but the first one takes time to prepare by studying the records of the various players, the characteristics of the opposing pitchers, the strategies favored by the two managers, and all the other nuances that may affect the outcome of the game. The second person just shows up on game day. It turns out to be an exciting game, and both people enjoy it. But the one who did the advance preparation enjoyed it to a greater depth. Yet the other spectator was not envious, because he had no way of understanding the deeper level of enjoyment being experienced by the one who did the advance preparation.

A similar comparison could be made in the context of an upcoming concert, an upcoming art exhibition, or any other sort of event. The rewards of attending any such event can vary a great deal between any two people without the slightest hint of envy creeping in. Perhaps heaven is arranged the same way. Everyone will be pleased to be there, even though no two people will be experiencing exactly the same rewards.

SUMMARY

Even for someone who rejects the historical evidence for the gospel accounts, the *structure* of Christianity's belief system can be defended as internally consistent and reasonable. The system offers a clear and sensible package: It identifies God's holiness and people's misbehavior. It comports with well-accepted standards of right and wrong. It holds people accountable for their actions. It offers all people a chance to succeed in spite of their misbehavior. And it eliminates uncertainty about where a person will spend his or her eternal future.

Many people will accept God's offer to have a lifetime relationship with him and then to spend eternity with him. But others will not. Some of them will remain skeptical or apathetic; some will procrastinate; and some will persist in their assumption that good deeds are an adequate ticket to heaven. But one thing is certain: Even though many people will reject it, God's passport of grace makes conceptual sense.

PROPHECY'S POSTSCRIPT

Most of us are more willing to accept the historical reality of an event that fits into a chain of earlier events than we are if the event only appears as an isolated blip on history's radar screen.

In the case of the Gospels, the chain is between Jesus of Nazareth and the prophetic hints about him written by Old Testament authors many centuries earlier. Some of the hints are vague, but others are quite clear. Three examples ought to suffice.

First, the prophet Isaiah, writing around 700 B.C., predicted that the messiah would come like a "shoot" from the "stump" of Jesse (the father of King David).[22] When David's kingdom was later destroyed by the Babylonians in 586 B.C., the aptness of Isaiah's chopped-tree metaphor was validated. More importantly, however, Jesus' own family tree did indeed turn out to include Jesse as one of the ancestors.[23]

Second, the prophet Micah, writing about the same time as Isaiah, identified Bethlehem as the place where the messiah would be born.[24] This is precisely the little town in which Mary gave birth to Jesus.[25]

Third, many centuries before the era of Roman crucifixion, and long before the lifetime of Jesus, King David uttered an anguished

---

[22] Isaiah 11:1.
[23] Matthew 1:6; Luke 3:31–32.
[24] Micah 5:2.
[25] Matthew 2:1; Luke 2:4.

prayer. In it he lamented what was being done to him by his enemies, who pierced his hands and feet and who cast lots for his clothing.[26] This prayer is eerily prophetic of what later happened to Jesus on the cross, when his hands and feet were nailed and his garments were gambled away to Roman soldiers.[27] It is also the source of Jesus' agonized plea from the cross for a reason why God had forsaken him.[28]

For many people, these kinds of Old Testament predictions are powerful evidence for the truth of the New Testament gospels. For others, the matter is not nearly so clear. Perhaps the most that can be agreed on, in this chapter about the common sense of Christianity, is that the Old Testament prophetic writings are consistent with, and can provide ancient illumination of, the gospel accounts.

---

[26] Psalm 22:16–18.

[27] Matthew 27:35; Mark 15:24; Luke 23:34; John 19:23–24.

[28] Psalm 22:1; Matthew 27:45–46; Mark 15:34.

Chapter Ten

✝

IMPEDIMENTS TO A CHRISTIAN FAITH

This chapter is addressed to people for whom the evidence is reasonably persuasive and for whom Christianity makes fairly good sense, but who still resist the impulse to take a step of faith because they have specific criticisms of Christian theology, churches, or individuals. Although poised at the threshold, they decline to step into faith because they don't like what they see up ahead. The Christian path seems to be blocked by insurmountable barriers, six of which we will now examine. Not all the barriers can be moved completely aside, but their negative effect can at least be opened up to serious debate.

CHRISTIANITY IS INTOLERANTLY EXCLUSIVE AND ELITIST

This is perhaps the most common obstacle to a step of Christian faith. It rests on the impression that Christianity is arrogant. And, to put the matter bluntly, individual Christians sometimes do project that attitude—a patronizing posture of intolerance. This demeanor hardly appeals to non-Christians. So Christians ought to avoid bludgeoning skeptics with judgmental and condescending pronouncements. Instead, they should display respect, gentleness, and humility. But, at the same time, skeptics should not expect Christians to deny the principles of their faith as recorded in the New Testament.

These principles can create enormous problems when they bump up against the culture of a modern pluralistic society. The difficulty arises because Jesus was the *only* founder of a major religion who claimed deity for himself (and who then demonstrated it by being resurrected from the dead). No other religious founder made such a claim—not Buddha, not Mohammed, not Confucius, not any of them. Nor do their followers make any such claim, emphasizing instead the *teachings* of their *dead* founders. By contrast, Christians emphasize the *identity* of their *resurrected* founder.

Thus Christians are compelled to walk a delicate line: They must proclaim the deity of Jesus without disparaging the founders of other faiths. To put it the other way around, Christians cannot apologize for the principles of their faith just to show tolerance for other religions. The delicacy of this line carries great potential for perceived Christian arrogance.

The core of the problem is contained in Jesus' unequivocal claim:

> *I* am the way and the truth and the life. No one comes to the Father except through *me*.[1]

> Whoever acknowledges me before men, I will also acknowledge him before my Father in heaven. But whoever disowns me before men, I will disown him before my Father in heaven.[2]

Jesus was not saying that adoption of his "approach to life" is the path. Nor was he saying that adherence to his "pattern of conduct" is the path. Rather, he was emphasizing that acknowledgment of him, *as a person*, is the sole path to God. According to Jesus, there is no other path. His language was plain, and his clarity is reinforced by the unambiguous context in which he spoke.[3] No matter how elitist it sounds, and no matter how many difficult questions

---

[1] John 14:6 (emphasis added). The point is amplified in the next section of this chapter. In addition, Paul formulated Jesus' claim as follows: "[I]f you confess with your mouth, 'Jesus is Lord,' and believe in your heart that God raised him from the dead, you will be saved." Romans 10:9.

[2] Matthew 10:32–33 (emphasis added).

[3] See John 14:1–11.

it raises,[4] this is the language that Jesus used. His statements were *not* formulated by later Christians—not by pastors in pulpits, not by scholars in schools, and not by parishioners in pews. Jesus proclaimed the principles himself, and the Christian's role is to abide by them. This may seem imperious, but Christians simply cannot rewrite the rules. And skeptics should not expect them to do so.

However, in explaining the exclusivity of their faith, Christians should not present themselves as superior and judgmental elitists. Rather, they need to emulate Jesus' own behavior. Christians' faith demands that they exhibit humility, relying on things like evidence, not arrogance, when describing God's passport of grace.[5] A Christian's message, if it is consistent with the faith, avoids any hint of moral superiority, since Christians, like everyone else, have fallen short in God's eyes. They should deliver a positive message about the certainty of a Christian's future, not a negative threat about everyone else's condemnation in the figurative fires of eternal hell.

The issue of Christian arrogance leads directly to the underlying question that was reviewed in chapter nine: Why would a loving God set up a system of exclusive access through Jesus? Why wouldn't he arrange things so that *all* people would receive an equal opportunity to have a relationship with him and to spend eternity with him? Why would he reject all those who had never heard the Christian message?

The flippant response is that God could do it any way he wanted. He could have chosen to bestow his grace only upon women, or only upon people over fifty, or only upon people with black hair, or only upon people who satisfied some similar criterion. But he didn't devise any such system. Instead, he simply designated Jesus

---

[4] Questions like: Why should God deny access to heaven for people of other faiths who have lived exemplary lives? What happens after death to people who lived exemplary lives before Jesus was born, e.g., Old Testament figures? Why didn't God offer salvation by more than one path? And questions that are somewhat more general, like: If "hell" exists, what is it like? If Satan exists, why does God allow him to continue?

[5] See 1 Peter 3:15.

as the passport. It is certainly true that this was God's own business and that people really don't have the right to question him. But we need to dig deeper than this sort of shallow answer.

The key point, as noted in chapter nine, is that God abhors wrongful acts. Unless he views a person through the lens of Jesus, God cannot have an eternal relationship with anyone who commits such acts. All people, as free moral beings, have the opportunity to comply with whatever moral law is taught by their culture and is written on their consciences. But Christianity adopts the realistic assumption that nobody, other than Jesus, ever chose to do so 100 percent of the time. Christianity understands that *all* people deviate from perfect compliance. So *nobody* can legitimately complain if God refuses to allow him or her into eternal fellowship. Nor can he or she legitimately complain if God sets up a system in which Jesus is the sole passport, even though many "good" people will never be exposed to his message. The plain fact is that none of us—not even people who never hear the message—has any inherent right to receive God's grace, to have a relationship with him, and to spend eternity with him.

The message of God's grace has been disseminated through the mouths and pens of individual Christians during the many centuries since Jesus' crucifixion. The hundreds of millions of people who hear or read the message have a free choice to either accept or reject God's grace. It is perfectly true that many people never hear the message. But their failure to enter into an eternal relationship with God is caused by their own choices to sometimes violate the moral law of their culture or their individual consciences.[6] It is not attributable to their failure to hear or read the New Testament message. As pointed out by one prominent Christian scholar:

> What does happen to the innocent person who has never heard of Christ?

---

[6] See Paul's analysis in Romans 2:14–15.

The assumption of innocence often slips into the question unnoticed. What is often meant is not a perfect innocence, but a relative innocence. . .

The New Testament makes it clear that people will be judged according to the light that they have. . .[T]hey do have a law "written on their hearts". . .

Thus if a person in a remote area has never heard of Christ, he will not be punished for that. What he will be punished for is the. . .disobedience to the law that is written in his heart.[7]

To summarize, skeptics need not be deterred by the Christian belief that God provided only a single way to receive his passport of grace. The plain fact of the matter is that God was under no obligation to set up any system at all for making passports available throughout a world filled with people who do not deserve them.

This leads us to the related question of why God would allow misbehaving Christians into heaven, when non-Christians who led exemplary lives are excluded.

CHRISTIANS DON'T PRACTICE WHAT THEY PREACH

People sometimes resist a step of faith because they perceive that Christian churches are full of hypocrites and misbehaving people. Sadly, they have a point. Some Christians certainly do make a habit of violating the standards of conduct that Jesus taught. Others conform to his standards outwardly, while secretly denying any faith in him. So their "faith" is not genuine, which means they are not true Christians.

However, none of this weakens the truth of Christianity. It only highlights the fact that all people are sinners—even the genuine Christians, who hold God's passport of grace and are therefore forgiven. But we must remember that forgiveness does not immunize

---

[7] Taken from *Reason to Believe* by R. C. Sproul, pp. 48–56. Copyright © 1978 by G/L Publications. Used by permission of Zondervan Publishing House. Available at your local bookstore or by calling 800-727-3480.

Christians from temptation. On the contrary, their Christian motivation is continually engaged in battle with their human desires. Yet even on those occasions when their motivation is overpowered by their desires, God's forgiveness will remain intact.

The Christian faith is based squarely and solely on the gospel claim that Jesus of Nazareth is God. The truth of the faith does not depend on the willingness of any person or group, past or present, to consistently measure up to God's standards. All Christians have fallen short—some more than others. The great strength of Christianity is the two-pronged way it deals with such failures: first, by providing forgiveness to repentant people who have fallen short, and, second, by motivating them to do better next time.

Hypocrisy, the profession of a belief that one does not truly hold, describes people who claim to be Christians but who do not truly believe that Jesus was God in human form and was resurrected from the dead. Some are secret hypocrites, who carefully conceal their disbelief. Others make no effort to keep it a secret, being unmasked by open behavior that violates Christianity's standards of conduct at every turn.

Hypocrites can be difficult to identify, especially those who avoid flagrant non-Christian conduct. Fortunately, however, judging people's faith is God's job—not ours—although most of us find it hard to refrain from judging individuals whose conduct cries out for condemnation. Even Paul, writing about people who "claim to know God, but by their actions they deny him," judgmentally described them as "detestable, disobedient and unfit for doing anything good."[8] The apostle John also condemned improper conduct:

> The man who says, "I know him [Jesus]," but does not do what he commands is a liar. . .Whoever claims to live in him must walk as Jesus did.[9]

---

[8] Titus 1:16. The importance of proper conduct is also described in James 2:14–24.
[9] 1 John 2:4–6.

These are strong indictments. But we need to remember that they apply to imperfect individuals in a human society, not to the Christian faith itself as described in the New Testament. The misbehaving individual may be a minister, a leading member of a congregation, a quiet member who always sits in a rear pew, or any other person who professes to be a Christian. The misbehavior may be adultery, alcoholism, manipulating and hurting other people, holding grudges, or any other non-Christian conduct. But no such conduct by any such person can erode the truth of Jesus' message, any more than a manufacturer's claim to produce the best electric razor is invalidated just because some of its employees use competing brands.

The lesson is clear: True Christians whose conduct often contradicts their Christian principles can be rated as detestable and disobedient within the context of human society. Professing Christians who are secretly skeptical can be rated as hypocrites. But people who are troubled by the presence of misbehaving Christians and hypocrites in the church can take comfort in the fact that God alone will judge the eternal destiny of both groups. He will identify the hypocrites and deny them a passport of grace. Similarly, he will identify the true, repentant Christians, whose conduct is occasionally abominable. They will receive his passport of grace, although their rewards in heaven will be different than the rewards for Christians who have diligently tried—sometimes unsuccessfully—to follow Jesus' standards throughout their human lives.[10]

In the meantime, nobody ought to refuse the step of faith just because he or she doesn't want to associate with churchgoing sinners and hypocrites. Nor should a person refuse the step of faith just because he or she does not wish to be an heir to whole groups of misbehaving Christians in bygone eras, such as the people who participated in American witch trials, in European heresy trials, and in excesses of the medieval Crusades. None of this terrible conduct—this hypocrisy—destroyed the truth of the Christian

---

[10] See pp. 175–177.

faith. It merely illustrated the extent to which professing Christians can go astray.

A person's eternal destiny is far more important than worrying about the misconduct of earlier eras and staying away from some offensive people who may inhabit the pews on Sunday morning. Rejecting God's passport of grace for this sort of criticism makes about as much sense as throwing away a Super Bowl ticket just because a few of the fans will hypocritically root against their favorite team after betting money on its opponent.

JESUS WAS A WISE TEACHER AND FINE ROLE MODEL, BUT HE WAS NOT GOD

This viewpoint constitutes another familiar barrier to a step of Christian faith. Some people adopt it because they doubt that Jesus really claimed to be God. Others adopt it because they are biased against the possibility of supernatural events. They can readily accept the historical truth of observable events described in the Gospels, and they may concede that some sort of impersonal God actually exists, but they balk at any notion of a *personal* God who literally came to Earth as a human being.

All these people take refuge in the drab notion that Jesus was merely a man of high moral standards who taught wisely about human values and conduct (although they sidestep the question of why the teachings of such a harmless man would have incurred the relentless wrath of the Jewish authorities). For people who have adopted this viewpoint, a step of faith will require a review of what Jesus reportedly said about himself.

Did Jesus claim to be God? All four New Testament gospels record statements by Jesus that bear on the issue of his divinity. Collectively, they are persuasive that Jesus personally believed he was God. He may have been wrong, but this is certainly what he believed. Sometimes he directly claimed identity with God. Sometimes he indirectly implied identity with God. And sometimes he asserted the same authority as God. About a dozen examples should suffice:

I and the Father are one.[11]

When Jesus made this statement to a group of Jews at the temple, they began stoning him "for blasphemy, because you, a mere man, claim to be God."[12]

Anyone who has seen me has seen the Father.[13]

[T]he high priest said to him [Jesus]. . ."Tell us if you are the Christ, the Son of God." "Yes, it is as you say," Jesus replied.[14]

The high priest responded by labeling Jesus' statement as blasphemous, a clear recognition that Jesus was claiming deity.

No one has ever gone into heaven except the one who came from heaven—the Son of Man [a name Jesus used for himself].[15]

This statement is similar to one of Jesus' prayers, in which he refers to "the glory I had with you [God] before the world began."[16]

You [Jesus' Jewish audience] are from below; I am from above. You are of this world; I am not of this world. I told you that you would die in your sins; if you do not believe that I am [the one I claim to be], you will indeed die in your sins.[17]

---

[11] John 10:30. The Greek word that is translated "one" is neuter in gender. This seems to signify the concept of "essence."

[12] John 10:33.

[13] John 14:9.

[14] Matthew 26:63–64; a virtually identical colloquy appears in Mark 14:61–62, and a similar one is contained in Luke 22:70.

[15] John 3:13.

[16] John 17:5.

[17] John 8:23–24.

[B]efore Abraham was born, I am.[18]

This latter statement is structured with a peculiar juxtaposition of past and present tenses. In it, Jesus was identifying himself with God, who, according to the Old Testament, told Moses, "I AM WHO I AM," and instructed Moses to say to the Israelites, "I AM has sent me to you."[19]

> I tell you, whoever acknowledges me before men, the Son of Man [Jesus] will also acknowledge him before the angels of God. But he who disowns me before men will be disowned before the angels of God.[20]

> Then those who were in the boat worshipped him, saying "Truly you are the Son of God."[21]

According to the Old Testament, nobody other than God may be worshipped.[22] Jesus himself clearly understood this.[23] Yet he accepted worship.

> Jesus. . .said to the paralytic, "Son, your sins are forgiven."[24]

Only God has the authority to forgive sins. Yet Jesus did so on many occasions.

> I am the good shepherd.[25]

---

[18] John 8:58
[19] Exodus 3:14.
[20] Luke 12:8–9.
[21] Matthew 14:33. Other occasions of worship: Matthew 28:9, 17; Luke 24:52; John 9:38.
[22] Exodus 20:1–5; Deuteronomy 5:6–9.
[23] Matthew 4:10; Luke 4:8.
[24] Mark 2:5.
[25] John 10:11, 14.

In the Old Testament, God alone is referred to as his people's "shepherd."[26]

> I am the way and the truth and the life. No one comes to the
> Father except through me.[27]

In addition to these specific claims of divinity, Jesus regularly addressed God as "Father" when he was praying.[28] He used the Aramaic word *Abba*, which in modern English would be translated "dad" or "daddy."[29] Such an informal word would not have been used by Jewish people of that day. Jesus' adoption of an intimate, familial term was probably unheard of, thus reinforcing the conclusion that Jesus considered himself as deity.

When all of Jesus' claims about himself are assembled, it is difficult to dispute the conclusion that he did indeed believe he was God. Admittedly, he never said so in exactly those words. But that ought not to be surprising. Few modern corporate executives, for example, walk the office halls proclaiming their vice-presidential titles. Rather, when the occasion arises, they typically speak in such terms as their relationship to the chief executive officer, the extent of their authority, or how they plan to fulfill their responsibilities. Jesus spoke in the same way. He talked about his oneness with the Father, his authority to forgive sins and accept worship, and his responsibility as the gatekeeper on the path to heaven. Even though Jesus did not *explicitly* say, "I am God," he used words that clearly claimed his preexisting and eternal identity as God.

---

[26] Psalms 23:1.

[27] John 14:6.

[28] Luke 10:21, 23:46; Matthew 26:42; John 11:41; Mark 14:36.

[29] This Aramaic word is preserved in Mark's gospel (14:36). The other three gospels translate the word into Greek, thereby eliminating the exact word spoken by Jesus. Two of Paul's letters, written five or ten years before the earliest gospel, also preserve the word "Abba." Galatians 4:6 and Romans 8:15.

It can, of course, be argued that the original gospels are not to be trusted as accurate records of every detail. After all, they were written thirty to sixty years after Jesus' death. How could they have been completely accurate in transcribing the exact words that Jesus actually spoke, particularly since the authors undoubtedly condensed and rearranged much of what he said? The answers are three: First, Jesus' teachings were probably being compiled in writing at a very early date. Second, oral transmission in the Middle East culture of that day was very common and highly reliable. And, third, condensation and rearrangement would not have fundamentally altered Jesus' words or meanings, especially his pivotal and oft-repeated claim to be God.[30]

In addition to the gospel evidence, we know from secular literature that the early Christians considered Jesus to be God. Pliny, the Roman governor of Bithynia around A.D. 112, wrote that the Christians in his province habitually sang a hymn "to Christ as to a god."[31]

What are the logical options when evaluating Jesus' claim? Apart from the implausible notion of legend or myth, we have three possible ways to assess Jesus' claim of divinity: First, he actually believed it, but he was deluded. Second, he did not actually believe it, making him a liar. Or, third, he actually believed it, and it was true. There seem to be no other options.

What if Jesus was deluded about his divinity? How does that fit with the known facts? Not very well. It is hard to imagine that a man who was under such a massive delusion for at least his last three years on Earth would have been able to teach so profoundly about living a compassionate and successful human life. Jesus' teachings were psychologically sound. Nothing in the Gospels even hints that he engaged in deranged behavior or spouted gibberish. To the contrary, the whole record of his life describes a man who behaved with composure and taught with wisdom. From

---

[30] See pp. 61–66.
[31] Quoted in F. F. Bruce, *New Testament History*, p. 165.

the written record, Jesus seems to have been the very antithesis of a deluded man.

What if Jesus lied about his divinity? How does that square with the facts? Not well at all. It is utterly inconsistent with his teachings about moral conduct. In fact, it would constitute the very essence of *immoral* conduct, because Jesus would have been intentionally leading his followers astray in their own spiritual walk. Moreover, it would mean that Jesus was an extraordinarily foolish liar, because he would have knowingly volunteered for a Roman crucifixion. Finally, it does not fit at all with his resurrection. God would hardly have chosen a consummate liar to be the only person he ever resurrected from the dead and transformed into a different existence—an existence from which Jesus claimed to have originally come. The option of a lying Jesus is quite far-fetched.

So what is left? Only the third option. People with a strong antisupernatural bias may choke a bit, but a reasonable review of the options leads to the least unlikely explanation for Jesus' claim: It was true. He was indeed God in the flesh.

THE GOSPELS MAY BE TRUE, BUT THEIR MIRACLE STORIES ARE LEGENDS

Even a person who concedes the historical reliability of the Gospels in all other respects can doubt the accounts of Jesus' miracles—phenomena that were evidently aimed at authenticating Jesus' ministry and demonstrating God's compassion. Yet the concept of miracles is not inherently illogical, provided that an all-powerful God indeed exists. Nevertheless, many people do have a problem with them.

They can explain the various healing stories[32] as psychological cures for psychosomatic ailments. They can view the changing of water into wine[33] as an ancient version of a modern magician's trick, or perhaps as a mere symbolic story. The nature miracles,

---

[32] E.g., Mark 7:31–37; Luke 5:12–26; John 9:1–12.
[33] John 2:1–11.

like walking on water,[34] are dismissed out of hand or explained away as hallucinations. And the spectacular performance of feeding five thousand people with five small barley loaves and two small fish[35] is rationalized as Jesus' clever technique for encouraging those people in the audience who had brought ample food to share it with the ones who had brought none. Jesus' alleged virgin birth[36] is simply ridiculed (and is even dodged by many Christians).

The net result is that some people decline to take the step of Christian faith because they just cannot accept the historical truth of the miracle stories. Having never witnessed a true miracle, and knowing that miracles, by definition, are unique events contrary to the laws of nature, these people deny that Jesus' miracles actually took place. So they resist the step of Christian faith.

At the outset, it will be helpful to agree that the mere fact someone has never personally encountered a miracle does not exclude the logical possibility that one could occur on his or her front lawn tomorrow. Obviously, it will not be likely. But past experiences in our lives cannot be projected into the future with 100 percent certainty. A person who has spent his entire life on an isolated tropical island would be mystified by a natural phenomenon like ice. Never having experienced anything like it in his life, he would surely deny that water had ever been transformed into a solid object. The most he might concede is the mere logical possibility.

So it is with the gospel miracles. They are logically possible, even though no physical evidence is available to confirm or refute them. The only independent evidence is literary. The Jewish historian Josephus wrote that Jesus was a "doer of wonderful works,"[37] which probably means that he performed miracles as a way of demonstrating his divinity.

---

[34] Matthew 14:22–33.
[35] John 6:1–15; Mark 6:30–44.
[36] Luke 2:1–14.
[37] "The Antiquities of the Jews" 18.63–64, *The Works*, p. 480.

Apart from Josephus, we must fall back on the face value presumption that the Gospels should be considered factually accurate unless there is reason to think they are factually false. In the case of ordinary human events, this sturdy presumption is easy to apply. But the miracle stories are somehow different. People can readily succumb to an antisupernatural viewpoint and thus reject the presumption entirely.

Only one argument seems to be available as a substitute for direct evidence of the miracle stories. It goes like this: If Jesus' claim to divinity is true, it leads to the conclusion that God exists. By definition, God is supernatural and is therefore capable of performing the kinds of events we call "miracles." The only miracle for which we have any evidence is his supernatural action in resurrecting Jesus from the dead.[38] But if God was capable of performing this one miraculous act, then he was certainly capable of bringing about Jesus' birth in a miraculous fashion and later empowering the human Jesus to perform all the miraculous acts recorded in the four gospels.

So if one miracle by God—Jesus' resurrection—is attested by the Gospels and by some independent evidence, it should not be extraordinarily difficult to accept the reality of the earlier miracles, especially since they were performed by the very person who was later resurrected.

A GOOD GOD WOULD NOT ALLOW SUFFERING AND EVIL IN THE WORLD

The world is full of good people. But they are often forced to suffer, sometimes at the hands of other people (from genocidal tyrants to small-time criminals), sometimes as a result of natural events (from hurricanes to diseases), and sometimes because of technological failures (from airplane crashes to dam failures). So the question inevitably arises: Why would a good God allow so much unfair, random suffering in the world? For some people this difficult and paradoxical question, to which the Bible provides no

---

[38] See chapters seven and eight.

crystal-clear answers, impedes their step of Christian faith. Of course, the matter can be turned around by asking skeptics the opposite question: If the world is godless, how do we account for *good* moral qualities, like love, generosity, and self-sacrifice?

Sensible responses to the problem of suffering are elusive, but even partial explanations can provide illumination. However, a suffering person is seldom helped by remarks like, "God is trying to teach you something" or, "Your faith just isn't strong enough." Such accusatory statements usually sound hollow and normally are counterproductive. Besides, nobody has any real way of knowing whether they are true or false. Most suffering people would be better served by an honest, straightforward comment like, "Life can just be unfair."

The problem of suffering and evil can be put into context by recognizing three points. First, people, not God, are the ones who misbehave. God allows it, but he does not directly cause it. Second, a "good" God is not the same as a "kind" God. A "kind" God would want nothing more than to see his people constantly happy and free from suffering. But this would require him to endlessly intervene in human affairs, thereby eliminating human choice—a vital component of humanity itself. He seems to have declined this approach. Instead, wanting his people to experience more than mere kindness, he became a "good" God, giving people the opportunity to grow and mature, sometimes through adversity. Third, the human life of every person will eventually come to an end. No matter how often our physical ailments are healed, each of us will die of something, sometime. On an eternal time scale—the one in which Christians believe—a human life span is but the blink of an eye, whether it lasts ten days or ten decades. It is simply a prologue to life eternal.

We shall first look at the issue of good people who suffer at the hands of another person's evil or careless conduct. The most sensible explanation for such suffering boils down to this: God created people with the capacity for moral growth and for loving relationships with each other and with him. Jesus confirmed this principle when he taught the Pharisees that the first and greatest commandment was to "love the Lord your God with all your heart and with all your soul and with all your mind" and that the second commandment was to "love your neighbor as yourself."[39] This sort of love cannot be coerced. It must be voluntarily chosen. So God could have accomplished his objective of loving relationships and moral growth in no other way than by giving people the free will to *choose* them. Yet free will automatically created the risk that people would sometimes misbehave, choosing evil or careless conduct rather than good and careful conduct.[40] God had no way of avoiding this risk without abolishing his gift of free will. To eliminate the possibility of evil behavior would have destroyed the very freedom with which God had endowed his people. So he declined to create a race of sinless robots, incapable of voluntarily choosing moral conduct and genuine love. Instead, he chose to create a race of human beings who were free to choose either good behavior, such as the love bestowed by caring parents on a newborn infant, or bad behavior, such as the reckless driving of the drunken person who kills the infant.

Thus half of the original question can be plausibly answered: A "good" God can indeed allow evil human behavior into the world, because it is a necessary outcome of the free will that he chose to bestow upon the entire human race.

But the other half of the question still remains: How can a "good" God allow the human suffering caused by natural events or technological failures? This is a somewhat harder issue, involving infinitely complex scenarios. And it inevitably raises the question of how and when God should selectively suspend natural laws, such as the force of gravity that is tugging at a plummeting air-

---

[39] Matthew 22:37–39.

[40] Admittedly, this statement does not explain how God's people, whom he originally created as good, first became inclined to occasionally choose evil conduct. The answer probably lies along the line that the very essence of *choice* is the opportunity to freely select between two categories of conduct: good and bad. Without that opportunity, there cannot be choice in the first place.

plane. Perhaps the most perceptive answer is one articulated by a Seattle pastor:

> I think it likely that frequent miracles would make us all quite careless. If we could be assured that God would always intervene and change the course of nature to our advantage, we would never learn self-discipline and self-control. We would never learn dependence upon Him. We would not even take death seriously enough to prepare for it. God, in His ultimate wisdom and compassion, must ration His miracles, granting just enough to assure us that He is indeed the source of them all, while at the same time keeping us from presuming upon His constant intervention. . .Whether we recover from a particular operation or disease is utterly inconsequential in comparison to whether we receive eternal life through casting ourselves upon His care. That is the only miracle in which He is ultimately interested. . .
>
> All our experiences of pain and suffering and fear and confusion and discontent. . .prepare us to accept Christ's ultimate solution. Should He relieve those circumstances in advance, it is likely that we would never give ourselves wholly to Him—the singular act which assures us of participation in that final miracle.[41]

This answer is built on the premise that human lives are fleeting when compared with eternal life. It states that each person's personal sufferings are ultimately answered by Jesus, who does not offer a way to *escape* life's unfair sufferings, but who does provide a way to get *through* them. And he does so with the compassion of a man whose terrible hours on the cross taught him first hand what human suffering was all about.

These responses to the problem of unfair suffering make a good deal of sense under Christian theology. They may well suffice for

---

[41] Paul Smith, *Jesus: Meet Him Again for the First Time* (Gresham, OR: Vision House Publishing, 1994), pp. 122–3. Quoted by permission of Vision House Publishing.

many skeptics. But for other skeptics, and even for some Christians, "I don't know" may be the only answer, in which case the entire subject will remain a mystery. However, the mystery ought not to seriously impede a person's acceptance of the gospel record about Jesus' divinity and God's existence. A lingering level of uncertainty about unfair human suffering need not deter a step of faith by a person who is satisfied with the firm evidentiary foundation for gospel reliability.

CHRISTIAN DENOMINATIONS CONTRADICT EACH OTHER

Christianity exhibits a wide—and sometimes bewildering—diversity of opinion among its churches. For the skeptic, this can impede any serious consideration of becoming a Christian.

Christian differences, which occasionally lead to outright hostility, are a complex subject. But the essential components are not difficult to describe. They stem from two distinct—and almost conflicting—purposes served by the twenty-seven New Testament books: First, these books furnish the glue that holds the various Christian denominations together. Second, they define both ends of the Christian spectrum, leaving ample space for differences of interpretation and emphasis among the denominations. This range of permissible viewpoints has given Christianity an enduring strength—one that could not have been achieved with a monolithic structure under which many individual Christians would chafe and from which they would eventually want to depart.

Diverse theological opinions and emphases are nothing new. They have been a feature of Christianity from the very beginning. Jesus himself was born into a diversified Jewish culture, with its Pharisees, Sadducees, Essenes, and Zealots. We will touch on just a few historical examples of Christian disagreements.

The first great dispute arose in the first century A.D. It involved theological clashes between Jewish Christians (primarily in and around Jerusalem), who believed that Jewish law had to be followed in matters such as circumcision and dietary restrictions, and gentile Christians (primarily outside of Palestine), who did not believe that compliance with such laws was required.[42] Paul, whose missionary efforts in Asia Minor and Greece had given birth to many of the gentile Christian churches, was the leading proponent of the gentile position. He personally warned the church elders at Ephesus to be on guard against people among them who would "arise and distort the truth in order to draw away disciples after them."[43] This controversy, during the first few decades after Jesus' crucifixion, shows that the early church was far from a serene, idyllic movement. It also illustrates the kind of dispute that can take place *within* the boundaries of the Christian spectrum, as distinct from the kind that go *beyond* those boundaries (like whether Jesus was truly resurrected from the dead).

The next great debate erupted in the second century, when Gnosticism crept into the church from various philosophical and religious views of the time. Essentially, Gnosticism assumed the existence of a sharp dividing line between matter and spirit, claiming that Jesus was a pure spirit who entered the body of a man but who was never really human. Unlike the first-century dispute, this controversy involved a belief system that challenged the very core of Christianity: Jesus' identity. It was outside the boundaries of the Christian spectrum, and Gnosticism was rejected by the early church fathers.

Another major disagreement developed during the ensuing centuries, after the Roman Catholic Church had become the preeminent Christian church around the Mediterranean. Differences began to arise between the bishop of Rome (the pope) and the eastern bishops. Finally, in A.D. 1054, the slowly developing schism was made permanent. This resulted in creation of the Orthodox Church, based in Constantinople (modern Istanbul). The main point at issue had been the authority of the Roman pope, whose primacy was rejected by the Orthodox bishops. When the armies

---

[42] See Galatians 2:11–16.
[43] Acts 20:30.

of the Fourth Crusade sacked Constantinople in A.D. 1204, the breach was further solidified. It persists to this day.

A second major dispute with the Roman Catholic Church was manifested in the Protestant Reformation. Although the roots went back a century or two earlier, it is usually dated from October 31, 1517, when Martin Luther nailed to the church door in Wittenberg, Germany, his ninety-five points of dispute with Rome. In them he criticized many church practices as being contrary to the New Testament scriptures. Similar arguments were being put forth at about the same time by other priests and pastors around Europe. The Reformation movement spread rapidly, and today's Protestant churches are the result.

Even the Reformation itself was subject to divisive disputes. For example, Luther differed vigorously with his Swiss counterparts, Ulrich Zwingli and John Calvin, over the exact nature of the communion celebration. Because of such differences, today's Lutheran churches are a separate denomination from the Reformed/Presbyterian churches.

The multitude of divisive controversies over many centuries fragmented Christianity into the Roman Catholic Church, the various Orthodox churches, and the wide array of Protestant denominations. The key question today is whether all these schisms should be a stumbling block for anyone contemplating a step of Christian faith. The answer is emphatically no. In fact, the situation can well be viewed from the opposite perspective: Christianity's very diversity is a source of strength, because it provides a multitude of options for anyone who is trying to find a church home.

Differences among Christian denominations and individual Christian churches seldom involve a central teaching of the New Testament. Rather, the differences are typically about tangential matters, like differing forms of church government, disagreements over the relative importance and the meanings of certain scriptural texts, variations in the formality and details of liturgical practices, and divergent attitudes about Christianity's role in cultural, social, and political matters. Such disagreements vary in importance. But they do not undermine the core of Christianity. All mainline denominations are built on a foundation of the New Testament's central teachings, which include a faith in Jesus and his resurrection, a belief that salvation comes only through him, and a recognition of the importance of such sacraments as baptism in Jesus' name and periodic celebration of his Last Supper (communion meal).

At its bedrock level, the Christian faith is an individual's one-to-one relationship with God. Its fundamental doctrines spring from the New Testament, not from the practices of any particular church or denomination. The essential point was summed up by Paul, who (as we noted in earlier chapters) wrote that:

> if you confess with your mouth, "Jesus is Lord," and believe in your heart that God raised him from the dead, you will be saved.[44]

Peter formulated his own summary:

> Salvation is found in no one else [than Jesus], for there is no other name under heaven given to men by which we must be saved.[45]

Such statements are the cornerstone of every Christian person's faith and of every Christian church's mission. Christianity's great strength is its insistence on these fundamental tenets. They hold all individual Christians together, and they set the boundaries for various denominational menus. Each individual Christian can choose the menu of a particular denomination or church that best suits his or her personal preference and comfort level. All the while he or she can rest secure in the basic Christian truths being offered on that menu.

---

[44] Romans 10:9.
[45] Acts 4:12.

CONCLUSION

Christianity, even for those who intellectually accept its historical truth, still requires a step of faith. A person can refuse to take that step by capitulating to impediments like the six discussed in this chapter. But he ought not to turn away from faith without first evaluating the significance and the potency of whatever particular impediments are gnawing at him. The eternal consequences of bypassing such an evaluation could be enormous.

Epilogue: After Faith, What Next?

✝

Let us assume that a skeptical person

- has embarked on a search for answers to the questions about God and heaven,
- has investigated the historical Jesus of Nazareth,
- has concluded that the New Testament gospels accurately record Jesus' birth, life, teachings, death, and resurrection, and
- has then taken a genuine step of faith.

If all these things have occurred, what happens next?

At the outset, the person must enter into a transaction with God, by telling God in prayer that he or she (1) acknowledges past sinful conduct and resolves to turn away from it, (2) believes that God raised Jesus from the dead, and (3) places full trust in Jesus as the one who will henceforth direct his or her life. The particular words used in such a prayer are unimportant. Rather, the importance flows from the person's sincerity in openly confessing to God his or her innermost thoughts and feelings. Once the prayer has been offered, God will confirm the transaction by giving the person his passport of grace. No outward sign of the transaction is likely to burst upon the scene. But, in modern parlance, it will be a "done deal."

Having accepted the passport of grace, the former skeptic is now assured of an eternal relationship with God. But does this make any practical difference in his or her remaining life on Earth? Or, to turn the question around, should the former skeptic simply bask in the assurance of eternity with God while continuing unabated in his or her previous lifestyle? The answer is no. Shrugging one's shoulders and persisting in all the old ways may mean that the person's faith is false. If it is, then he will not spend eternity where he thinks he will. Only God and the person will know for sure.

If a person's Christian faith is genuine, then his future perspective and behavior will almost surely begin to change. His conduct will not always comport with his faith, but he will constantly be seeking to improve it, day-by-day, month-by-month, and year-by-year. God's standards will serve as his plumb line, unaffected by shifting secular values and attitudes.

Those standards are embedded as nuggets of information throughout the New and Old Testaments. This book is not the place to extract and compile them into a list of rules for Christian conduct. But it is the place to let interested skeptics catch a glimpse of what lies ahead if they do become Christians. A few examples should suffice.

In their interpersonal relationships, Christians are expected to accept one another, just as Jesus accepted each one of them.[1] No Christian should be self-righteously judgmental about another Christian's conduct or attitudes. To do so would run afoul of Jesus' own admonition: "Do not judge, or you too will be judged."[2] This does not require Christians to close their eyes to someone else's bad behavior. Instead, Jesus simply cautions Christians against puffing up their own egos by harboring a critical, petty, arrogant attitude toward others.

But mere acceptance of others is not enough. Christians are supposed to encourage,[3] serve,[4] and love[5] one another. By encouraging, they help another person develop the ability to accomplish his or her own goals. By serving, they directly assist the other person in achieving those goals. And by loving, they exhibit their genuine concern about the well being of the other person.

---

[1] Romans 15:7.

[2] Matthew 7:1.

[3] 1 Thessalonians 5:11.

[4] Galatians 5:13.

[5] 1 Corinthians 13.

The concept of Christian love can pose a difficult problem. How is a Christian supposed to "love" some self-centered, greedy scoundrel who has intentionally inflicted injury on the Christian? It's a tough thing to do. But the Christian must give it a try. Jesus himself, affirming a statement in the Old Testament, commanded Christians to love their neighbors as themselves.[6] He was not suggesting an option. He was issuing a mandate. But how does a Christian undertake to comply?

Perhaps a simple little distinction will help the medicine go down. Christians are indeed commanded to love everyone, even people who have hurt them. But Jesus nowhere commanded Christians to like such people. This distinction between "loving" and "liking" is not a word game. Rather, it highlights a vital principle: Christians can intensely dislike someone, but they must still love that person *because he or she is one of God's creations and has the potential to become better*. This principle is the essence of Christian outreach. Every Christian must exhibit love toward his unpleasant neighbors by continually offering his own conduct as a demonstration of what God's grace is all about.

Another aspect of the Christian's obligation to his neighbors is expressed in Paul's letter to the Philippians:

> Each of you should look not only to your own interests, but also to the interests of others.[7]

Christians should always balance their own self-interest against the self-interests of other people. Paul did not limit his statement to particular situations. It applies in family relationships, friendship relationships, economic and business relationships, and even conduct toward strangers. In every arena of human activity, Christians should take into consideration the interests of everyone involved, including themselves.

---

[6] Matthew 22:39; Mark 12:31; Luke 10:27–28.
[7] Philippians 2:4.

In a nutshell, Christians are to avoid greed and self-indulgence.[8] Their faith should equip them to live lives permeated by love, joy, peace, patience, kindness, goodness, faithfulness, gentleness, and self-control.[9] Each of these qualities ought to characterize the Christian life.[10]

And lest anyone think that the principles of Christian conduct are limited to the New Testament, the admonition against greed goes all the way back to the Old Testament book of Proverbs.[11] The Old Testament also provides us with an overarching scriptural standard:

> And what does the Lord require of you? To act justly and to love mercy and to walk humbly with your God.[12]

If every human being acted justly toward everyone else, exhibited mercy toward all people, and reverently embraced God as part of his or her life, planet Earth would be a far better place.

So Christianity involves compliance with God's rigorous requirements. But if that's all it amounted to, then skeptics might well shy away from a step of faith. Fortunately, however, Christianity offers much more than just rules and regulations. Through the nudging of God's Holy Spirit, Christian people are provided with deep and lasting rewards during life on Earth—rewards that may seem esoteric but that are nonetheless real.

To offer a personal example, my own Christian faith transformed a quick temper into quiet patience. It motivated me to stop using unseemly language. It diluted the pride and arrogance with which I sometimes viewed those people around me whose intelligence and education might have been a bit below my own. It imbued me

---

[8] Matthew 23:25; Luke 12:15; 1 Peter 5:2.

[9] Galatians 5:22–23.

[10] The qualities are well described and illustrated by Tim Riter in *Deep Down* (Wheaton, IL: Tyndale, 1995).

[11] Proverbs 15:27 and 28:25.

[12] Micah 6:8.

with tolerance for the differing opinions of others (while still defending my own views). It improved the gentleness with which I approached debates and controversies. And, at the deepest and most practical level, it equipped me to tap into the "peace of God, which transcends all understanding."[13] As Jesus himself said:

> Peace I leave with you; my peace I give you. I do not give to you as the world gives. Do not let your hearts be troubled and do not be afraid.[14]

As most people, I have faced some of life's problems. While coping with those that occurred after I had become a Christian, I derived a true sense of peace from the knowledge that, in the midst of things like a career crisis and my wife's health problems, God was working for my good and for hers.[15] This profound reservoir of support and guidance is available to every Christian. It may not be easy for skeptics to understand. But it is a real part of every Christian's life. Its benefits require nothing more than genuinely accepting God's passport of grace.

---

[13] Philippians 4:7.
[14] John 14:27.
[15] Romans 8:28.

Bibliography

Antonacci, Mark. *The Resurrection of the Shroud.* New York: M. Evans and Company, 2000.

Bailey, Kenneth E. "Middle Eastern Oral Tradition and the Synoptic Gospels." *Expository Times* 106 (1995): 363–367.

Behe, Michael J. *Darwin's Black Box.* New York: The Free Press, 1996.

Blaiklock, E. M. *The Archaeology of the New Testament.* Grand Rapids, MI: Zondervan, 1970.

Blomberg, Craig L. *The Historical Reliability of the Gospels.* Downers Grove, IL: Inter-Varsity, 1987.

Borkan, Marc. "Ecce Homo? Science and the Authenticity of the Turin Shroud." *Vertices–The Duke University Magazine of Science, Technology, and Medicine* Vol. X, No. 2 (Winter 1995): pp. 18–51.

Bruce, F. F. "Archaeological Confirmation of the New Testament." *Revelation and the Bible.* Ed. Carl F. H. Henry. Grand Rapids, MI: Baker, 1958.

Bruce, F. F. *The Books and the Parchments.* 4th ed. Old Tappan, NJ: Fleming H. Revell, 1984.

Bruce, F. F. *Jesus and Christian Origins Outside the New Testament.* Grand Rapids, MI: Eerdmans, 1974.

Bruce, F. F. *The New Testament Documents.* 5th rev. ed. Grand Rapids, MI: Eerdmans, 1994.

Bruce, F. F. *New Testament History.* New York: Doubleday, 1971.

Comfort, Philip Wesley. *The Origin of the Bible*. Wheaton, IL: Tyndale, 1992.

Comfort, Philip Wesley. *The Quest for the Original Text of the New Testament*. Grand Rapids, MI: Baker Book House, 1992.

Dunn, James D. G. *The Evidence for Jesus*. Louisville, KY: Westminster Press, 1985.

Eusebius. *The History of the Church*. Rev. ed. Trans. G. A. Williamson. London: Penguin Group, 1989.

Finegan, Jack. *The Archeology of the New Testament*. Rev. ed. Princeton, NJ: Princeton University Press, 1992.

France, R. T. *The Evidence for Jesus*. Downers Grove, IL: InterVarsity, 1986.

Geisler, Norman and Ron Brooks. *When Skeptics Ask*. Wheaton, IL: Victor Books, 1990.

Green, Michael. *The Day Death Died*. Downers Grove, IL: InterVarsity, 1982.

Greenhut, Zvi. "Burial Cave of the Caiaphas Family." *Biblical Archaeology Review* 18, No. 5 (September/October 1992): pp. 28–36.

Habermas, Gary R. *Ancient Evidence for the Life of Jesus*. Nashville, TN: Thomas Nelson, 1984.

Heller, John. *Report on the Shroud of Turin*. Boston: Houghton Mifflin, 1983.

Josephus, Flavius. *The Essential Writings*. Trans. and ed. Paul L. Maier. Grand Rapids, MI: Kregel, 1988.

Josephus, Flavius. *The Works*. New updtd. ed. Trans. William Whiston. Peabody, MA: Hendrickson, 1987.

Kersten, Holger & Elmar Gruber. *The Jesus Conspiracy*. Rockport, MA: Element Books, 1995.

Ladd, George Eldon. *I Believe in the Resurrection of Jesus*. Grand Rapids, MI: Eerdmans, 1975.

Lewis, C. S. *The Problem of Pain*. New York: Collier Books, 1962.

Little, Paul. *Know Why You Believe*. 3rd ed. Downers Grove, IL: InterVarsity, 1988.

Marino, Joseph. "The Shroud of Turin and the Carbon 14 Controversy." *Fidelity* (February 1989): pp. 36–45.

Martin, Ernest L. *The Star that Astonished the World*. 2d ed. Portland, OR: ASK Publications, 1996.

McDowell, Josh. *More Than a Carpenter*. Wheaton, IL: Living Books, 1986.

McDowell, Josh. *The Resurrection Factor*. San Bernardino, CA: Here's Life Publishers, 1981.

McDowell, Josh and Bill Wilson. *He Walked Among Us*. San Bernardino, CA: Here's Life Publishers, 1988.

McDowell, Josh and Bill Wilson. *A Ready Defense*. San Bernardino, CA: Here's Life Publishers, 1990.

McRay, John. *Archaeology and the New Testament*. Grand Rapids, MI: Baker Book House, 1991.

Metzger, Bruce M. *The Text of the New Testament*. 3d, enlarged ed. New York: Oxford University Press, 1992.

Montgomery, John Warwick. *History & Christianity*. Downers Grove, IL: InterVarsity, 1965.

Moreland, J. P. and Kai Nielsen. *Does God Exist?* Nashville, TN: Thomas Nelson, 1990.

Mosley, John. *The Christmas Star*. Los Angeles: Griffith Observatory, 1987.

Reich, Ronny. "Caiaphas Name Inscribed on Bone Boxes." *Biblical Archaeology Review* 18, No. 5 (September/October 1992): pp. 38–44.

Richardson, Cyril C., trans. and ed. *Early Christian Fathers*. New York: Macmillan, 1970.

Riter, Tim. *Deep Down*. Wheaton, IL: Tyndale, 1995.

Robinson, J. A. T. *Redating the New Testament*. London: SCM Press, 1976.

Romer, John. *Testament*. New York: Henry Holt, 1988.

Sanders, E. P. *The Historical Figure of Jesus*. London: Allen Lane, Penguin Press, 1993.

Smith, Paul. *Jesus: Meet Him Again for the First Time*. Gresham, OR: Vision House Publishing, 1994.

Sproul, R. C. *Reason to Believe*. Grand Rapids, MI: Zondervan, 1982.

Stanley, Charles. *Eternal Security*. Nashville, TN: Oliver-Nelson Books, 1990.

Stevenson, Kenneth E. and Gary R. Habermas. *Verdict on the Shroud*. Wayne, PA: Banbury Books, 1982.

Stevenson, Kenneth E. and Gary R. Habermas. *The Shroud and the Controversy*. Nashville, TN: Thomas Nelson, 1990.

Stott, John R. W. *Basic Christianity*. 2d ed. Downers Grove, IL: Inter-Varsity, 1971.

Strange, James F. and Hershel Shanks. "Synagogue Where Jesus Preached Found at Capernaum." *Biblical Archaeology Review* IX, No. 6 (November/December 1983): pp. 24–31.

Strobel, Lee. *The Case for Christ*. Grand Rapids, MI: Zondervan, 1998.

Suetonius, Gaius Tranquillus. *The Twelve Caesars*. Rev. ed. Trans. Robert Graves. London: Penguin Group, 1979.

Tacitus, P. Cornelius. *The Annals and The Histories*. Vol. 15 of Great Books of the Western World. Trans. Alfred John Church and William Jackson Brodribb. Chicago: Encyclopaedia Britannica, 1952.

Thiede, Carsten Peter and Matthew D'Ancona. *Eyewitness to Jesus*. New York: Doubleday, 1996.

Tzaferis, Vassilios. "Crucifixion—The Archaeological Evidence." *Biblical Archaeology Review* XI, No. 1 (January/February 1985): pp. 44–53.

Wild, Robert A. "The Shroud of Turin—Probably the Work of a 14th-century Artist or Forger." *Biblical Archaeology Review* X, No. 2 (March/April 1984): pp. 30–46.

Wilkins, Michael J. and J. P. Moreland, gen. eds. *Jesus Under Fire*. Grand Rapids, MI: Zondervan, 1994.

Wilson, Ian. *The Blood and the Shroud.* New York: The Free Press, 1998.

Wilson, Ian. *The Shroud of Turin.* Rev. ed. Garden City, NY: Image Books, 1979.

Witherington, Ben III. *The Jesus Quest.* Downers Grove, IL: InterVarsity, 1995.

Index

To order additional copies of

From

SKEPTIC *to*
CHRISTIAN

Have your credit card ready and call

Toll free: (877) 421-READ (7323)

or send 13.95* each plus $4.95 S&H**

to
WinePress Publishing
PO Box 428
Enumclaw, WA 98022

*Washington residents please add 8.4% tax.
**Add $1.00 S&H for each additional book ordered.